pedogogically

Messages & Myths

UNDERSTANDING
INTERPERSONAL COMMUNICATION

UNDERSTANDING INTERPERSONAL COMMUNICATION

Messages
and
Myths

DAN P. MILLAR, *Central Michigan University*

FRANK E. MILLAR, *Montana State University*

 ALFRED PUBLISHING CO., INC., NEW YORK

Copyright © 1976 by Alfred Publishing Co., Inc.
75 Channel Drive, Port Washington, N.Y. 11050

Printed and bound in the United States of America

Library of Congress Cataloging in Publication Data
Millar, Dan, 1938-
Messages and myths: understanding interpersonal
communication.

Bibliography: p.
1. Communication. 2. Interpersonal relations.
3. Nonverbal communication. I. Millar, Frank,
1944- joint author. II. Title.
P90.M476   301.14   75-33811
ISBN 0-88284-022-3

. . . To IRENE and FRANK
our MOM and POP

Contents

x

Preface

This book is built around a collection of communication myths we have come to live by. These myths prevent the development of an accurate picture of self and impair effective communication. We chose this structure for the book because human behavior grows, in large measure, out of a set of beliefs we have about ourselves, our environment and the people we contact. What we believe colors our expectations for social interaction, influencing our perception of ourselves, our messages, the recipients of those messages and the process of message sending and receiving. We cite academic research as well as some popular literature and poetry to help us describe and illustrate our points.

If we can demonstrate that the myths inhibit our giving and receiving love, accepting and being accepted and that they hinder our creation of a fully-functioning self, then the communication patterns fostered by the beliefs have reason to be identified and modified. We hope to achieve the identification and modification of these beliefs through a small, readable book which is self-sufficient. By readable, we mean intellectually sound but written with a conversational tone. We have tried to use enough examples, sufficient highlighting of the heavy content to assist the reader in retention, humor where appropriate, and reader-involvement techniques whenever possible.

Many textbook writers present their material as if it were *truth*. While it may be truth within a particular value frame, few authors present us with that value framework. By focusing upon myths (beliefs) we hope to pull out some of the values that underlie our communication patterns and show how they affect us. In this way we will try to reach individuals and to identify their beliefs and behaviors that interfere with the achievement of human development. Also, we see a need for a book that focuses upon the communication process within several settings as separate communication variables. For instance, we would like to write about the process and illustrate it by looking at communication patterns in love, the family, the dorm, rather than only look at small group communication in clinical or otherwise unrealistic environments.

Each chapter will identify the myth that is central to the chapter. A brief description of the myth will follow including the communication behavior associated with belief in the myth. The second portion of each chapter will analyze the substance of the myth from the perspective of current theoretic concepts regarding the myth under consideration. The third portion of each chapter will suggest ways to overcome the myth.

Occasionally we cite research or literature which we have labelled "Insights." We call this material insights because we feel it generally sheds light on some of the behavior the myths engender.

Our goals for this book are ambitious but reachable; and if some readers begin to make small advances toward caring about and achieving more effective communication, then we will have succeeded. And the credit for that success must be shared with our students, our colleagues and our families.

Introduction

Nothing we have tried to do is as difficult as what we're trying to do right now—to write our thoughts and feelings to you. We have never met you. There is no way for us to meet. You have no way of knowing us nor we you. The chance of us ever making contact is minimal, at best. But, we do want you to understand as much as possible what is said in this book.

Perhaps you'll agree with some of the analyses and conclusions, perhaps not. But, your agreement or disagreement is not as important as your understanding of the information transmitted. If you understand, you can take what is useful, refine what is ambiguous to you, and refute (not just evaluate) what you disagree with. The function of any book is to stimulate thought, not to dictate certainty. Hoping that you might better understand the book if you know some information about where our heads are, the following biographical and attitudinal sketches are presented.

DAN	*FRANK*
I'm a bit over 30 with a wife of 11 years and a son seven.	A bit? I am 30, had a wife for eight years but have been divorced for three. I have a son nine and a daughter six.

DAN	FRANK

There's a 90 pound black-saddled German shepherd lying on my feet, we call him Rusty.

A half-full tumbler of scotch with melted ice cubes rests on the arm of my chair.

The majority of joy, the majority of pain, the majority of peace, and the majority of my turmoil springs from those three.

My children taught me the meaning of love; and, more importantly, the feeling of love.

I live in a small Michigan town. From my front windows I look into farm lands that are now fallow but contain the homes of scores of meadowlarks, redwinged blackbirds, grackles, and a few dozen pheasants.

I live in a medium-sized city in Montana and from the front window of my apartment I see the snowcapped mountains.

The robins have built their second nest in the locust tree just off the patio. Mother robin is very distressed whenever I use my gas grill.

The family of cockroaches that live in my kitchen are very distressed whenever I clean.

As a youngster and young man I lived in a large midwestern city not far from Chicago and loved the pace and excitement of the big city.

Obviously, I also lived there, but I never got into it as my brother has described. Enjoyment instead of love and excitement, more accurately describes my feelings for the city.

As I aged, my thoughts have turned more to nature, to the peace of the country, to our

As I develop, my thoughts increasingly center on the need for increased acceptance of in-

DAN	*FRANK*
relationship with the natural world around us. But, I am glad that at some point in my life I had the opportunity to live in and around the big city.	dividual differences, on the value of compassion based on respect and trust—not tolerance and suspicion. The peace and beauty of our natural surroundings and the joy of being US are my principal "highs."
I was raised in a family of Democrats who voted independently. I am now an independent-voting Republican.	Ditto on Democrats. Dan and I disagree on the efficacy of the present situation as we see it, but we are both deeply committed to democratic ideals.
Even though I object to labeling people, it may be helpful for you to consider me a liberal in a conservative university and community.	I take a "liberal" stance on some issues and a "conservative" stance on others. Suffice it to say, as I only half-jokingly describe myself to students, that I'm trying to be sane in frequently insane situations.
I have always liked teaching, but I love watching people learn.	I love to stimulate learning by turning the classroom into a communication situation rather than an information-transmission one.

That is part of why we find writing a frustrating task—there is no way for us to know whether or not we have communicated. We can't know because we can't see or hear or feel your reactions. We can't know if we've been understood and if we've understood your responses. We'd much rather sit with you, face-to-face and talk. You sharing your thoughts with us, we sharing ours with you, with the hope that together we can arrive at some mutual understanding as to what was meant and felt; each respecting the thoughts and feelings of the other. But we can't, so what we have tried to do is write as if we were talking with you. We've tried, whenever possible, to use language that will be understood; to use language that will allow you to intellectually and emotionally get into what was written.

If the task of writing a book is so difficult and frustrating, why do we do it? We decided to write because we have been watching people struggle to relate to people, struggle to define themselves, and struggle to make contact with others in our highly interdependent, rapidly changing, symbolic world. This struggle for growth relationships, we all share. As we have watched and experienced these struggles, we've come to believe that at the core of this struggle is the ability to reach a communication state. Yet, tragically, much of our behavior prevents us from making interpersonal contact. A few can't because they lack the physical, intellectual and emotional capacities to do so. Most of us struggle because our communication behavior has been based upon a series of myths we hold about ourselves, about others, about the language we use, and the relationships we form. We can't invalidate these myths. We can say that they do not seem to be functional if one's goal is to live and become human, rather than "get through" life.

We have tried to identify some of these myths upon which much of our message behavior is based, to analyze them and offer alternatives. Our objective is to have these myths abandoned, believing that abandonment will encourage our freedom to become. Within this context, we hope that you will listen, not only to the words, but to the feelings.

To those of you who have not yet begun, as well as those who have, the struggle for more satisfying relationships, for identity, and for sanity, perhaps there will be some ideas expressed that will make your struggle easier. This won't make your growth less meaningful to you. But maybe we can help you avoid wasting energy by identifying some of the obvious pitfalls. In the long run, the goal is to become human. To be able to share in the joy of others with others; to be able to know self and change self; to be able to develop and change as a growing individual in an environment often hostile, sometimes frightening, constantly changing.

Communication can only take place within some context, but the process by which we reach a communication-state continually occurs in every interpersonal setting. If we were to look at the process in all possible contexts, the book would be much too long and tedious. We've attempted to organize the book around a series of myths we believe exist in our western society, myths that prevent us from developing meaningful human relationships. Within this framework, we've tried to usefully discuss the process of interpersonal transactions.

One last comment about us. As you read, if you think there is some humor, go ahead and smile, because it was probably intended.

To the hundreds of people, writers and students, who have stimulated and shaped our thoughts—thank you. But a specific and special thank you must go to Karen Millar (Dan's wife) who typed, edited, housed, fed, and adjudicated; to LuAnn Applegreen who typed the manuscript; and to John Stout, who encouraged us from the beginning.

Messages & Myths

UNDERSTANDING
INTERPERSONAL COMMUNICATION

1

COMMUNICATION DEFINED

MYTH
*"If I've Told You Once,
I've Told You a Hundred Times!"*

I overheard the following conversation between two university professors as I passed them in the hall.

"I'm sick and tired of this. You can repeat yourself until you're blue-in-the-face and nobody pays any attention. If I've told those students once, I've told them a hundred times to type their papers! But today, about half the class hands in handwritten papers and what scrawls!!"
"I know. They just don't pay any attention. You can communicate all you want to, but they still don't do what you ask. It gets harder and harder to come to class."

These teachers see the act of speaking to someone as communication. The words "speaking" and "communication" become synonymous in their eyes.

One day after a particularly super class, one woman began to cry. We talked and I discovered she was separating from her husband. Why? "We don't communicate anymore. Oh, we still talk. But there's no tenderness, no understanding, no compromise. Once . . . it was beautiful . . . If only we could've had this class five years ago!" She sees communication as a mutual understanding—as the rare moment when each participant knows that each understands and is understood by the other.

Unfortunately, a single word can have many meanings and communication is a word we all use—probably somewhat differently. Sometimes people mean, as did the teachers, the act and actions of speaking; sometimes, as did the woman, they mean mutual understanding (making a human connection). We conceptualize communication in the second way. That is, communication is more than sending messages, more than accurately receiving those messages. Both conditions are included, but the real key is the knowledge of each that the other has accurately received and interpreted the messages. Communication is both these conditions plus the knowledge of each participant that the other has, in fact, accurately received and interpreted the messages sent. Communication is not just sending/receiving; communication is responding. Communication is not just speaking, communication is listening. Communication, when mutual understanding occurs, is not a moment but a period in time—a state.

Now, we are not saying that accurate sending and receiving of messages is unimportant. The development of mutual understanding presumes accuracy (the best possible given symbols and our humanness). Further, in certain social settings and with certain persons, the seeking of mutual understanding and the relational requirements of such a state are inappropriate. Getting orders from your sergeant, social analysis from your history lecturer, the "state of the union" from the President, exemplify social settings in which the goal of mutual understanding is inappropriate. Information accurately transmitted and (hopefully) accurately received is the appropriate goal. Most of our waking activities demand accurate information exchange rather than understanding. However, the development of human relationships between people (not between social roles) does require understanding—a getting into the other. What seems to happen to people is that they can't tell the difference between the two —information exchange and communication. So they think of them as synonymous, which leads to the belief that telling equals communication.

This book attempts to analyze the process of communication, of creating a state of mutual understanding. Most of what we say has relevance to information exchange, for improving

4

our ability to send and receive messages enhances our chances for creating a communication-state with someone else. We cannot guarantee that our book will lead you to mutual understanding, but we can say that if all of us improve as message senders within the framework described in the following pages, the chances of being able to create a communication-state will be enhanced.

VIEWS OF OTHERS

Let's begin thinking about the occurrence and the process of communication by answering a few questions. Below are descriptions of situations in which people assume they find communication taking place. Please respond to each situation by determining "yes, communication has occurred"; "no, communication has not occurred"; or, "it depends, maybe it has and maybe it hasn't."

Occurrence of Communication

Situation	*Answers*		
The President speaks on national television to explain to the country why a certain foreign policy decision has been made.	Yes	No	It depends
You read this book or a newspaper or a magazine.	Yes	No	It depends
A teacher lectures to students on the advantages and disadvantages of a dissonance-theory approach to attitude change.	Yes	No	It depends
A girl at the beach winks at a handsome young man she has never met before.	Yes	No	It depends

Situation	*Answers*		
A boss explains to a new employee how to do the job.	Yes	No	It depends
A husband and wife discuss the family budget and whether or not they can afford a new car.	Yes	No	It depends
Representatives of management and labor sit around a table and negotiate the terms of an upcoming contract.	Yes	No	It depends
A salesman has just sold you something you hadn't intended to buy when you walked into the store.	Yes	No	It depends
You've just arrived in a strange town and asked a gas station attendant for directions. You have followed the directions given and arrived at your destination.	Yes	No	It depends
A friend of yours has just convinced you that it is socially irresponsible to have more than two children.	Yes	No	It depends

Whether you answered "yes," "no," or "it depends," depends upon how you define "communication."

Some people think of communication as occurring whenever an individual sees, hears, touches, tastes, or smells something. If another hears you speaking, then you have communicated; if taste buds tingle after the first bite of Beef Wellington, then the chef has communicated; if you see a novice skater slip and slide, arms flailing and legs flapping on the ice and laugh at the sight, then the skater has communicated; if the smell of the purple, blue, and yellow wild mountain flowers give you a "high," then you have communicated with nature. In these cases, any response to any stimuli is considered communication. Some communication scholars (communicologists) also think of communication in the same way (see Thayer, Insight 1.1, No. 9). If you think of communication as taking some stimuli into account, then for all of the situations, you would have answered "yes."

Some people think of communication as occurring whenever one person attempts to generate meaning in the mind of another person, with either language or action. Using this definition, we, as writers of this book, are communicating with you; when a black guy shrieks at a white sheriff, "You jivin' honkey!", he is communicating with the arresting officer; when a politician argues for support of a mass transportation program which you don't understand, then he is communicating with you. If you think of communication as the attempt to stimulate meaning (see McCroskey, Insight 1.1, No. 4), then for all of the situations, you would have answered "yes."

Other people think of communication as occuring whenever information (in the form of language or action) is transmitted from one place to another or from one person to another. Using this definition, writers communicate when their books are read; a computer communicates when it types a printout; a television announcer communicates when he presents the evening news. Some communicologists define communication in the same way, as a transmission of message (see Miller, Insight 1.1, No. 1, and Berlo, No. 6). If you think of communication in this manner, then for all of the situations, you would have answered "yes."

INSIGHT 1.1 Definitions of Communication

1. "Communication means that information is passed from one place to another." George A. Miller, *Language and Communication,* McGraw-Hill, New York, 1951, p. 6.

2. "The word communication will be used here in a very broad sense to include all of the procedures by which one mind may affect another." Warren Weaver, *The Mathematical Theory of Communication,* University of Illinois Press, Urbana, Ill., 1964, p. 3.

3. "Communication is a term used to refer to any dynamic, information-sharing process." Theodore Clevenger, "What is Communication?", *Journal of Communication*, 9, 1959, p. 5.

4. Communication is ". . . the process of one individual's stimulating meaning in the mind of another individual by means of a message." James C. McCroskey, *An Introduction to Rhetorical Communication*, Prentice-Hall, Englewood Cliffs, N.J., 1968, p. 21.

5. "Real communication occurs, . . . when we listen with understanding. What does this mean? It means to see the expressed idea and attitude from the other person's point of view, to sense how it feels to him, to achieve his frame of reference in regard to the thing he is talking about." Carl R. Rogers, *On Becoming a Person*, Houghton Mifflin, Boston, 1961, pp. 331–332.

6. "Communication is a process involving the transfer of matter-energy that carries symbolic information." David K. Berlo, unpublished mimeo, Michigan State University, 1969.

7. "Communication occurs whenever persons attribute significance to message-related behavior." C. David Mortensen, *Communication: The Study of Human Interaction*, McGraw-Hill, New York, 1972, p. 14.

8. Communication is ". . . an attempt to get meaning . . . communication is any effort to acquire understanding." John R. Wenburg and William W. Wilmot, *The Personal Communication Process*, John Wiley & Sons, New York, 1973, p. 7.

9. "Thus the phenomenon basic to and underlying every situation in which human communication occurs is simply this: that an organism (an individual) took-something-into-account, whether that something was something someone did or said or did not do or say, whether it was some observable event, some internal condition, the meaning of something being read or looked at, some feeling intermingled with some past memory—literally anything that could be taken-into-account by human beings in general and that individual in particular." Lee Thayer, *Communication and Communication Systems*, Richard D. Irwin, Inc., Homewood, Ill., 1968, pp. 26–27.

10. ". . . communication can be regarded in the broadest sense as a structural system of significant symbols (from all the sensorily based modalities) which permit ordered human interaction." Ray L. Birdwhistell, *Kinesics and Context*, University of Pennsylvania Press, Philadelphia, 1970, p. 95.

11. "The very word 'communicate' means 'share,' and inasmuch as you and I are communicating at this moment, we are one. Not so much as a union as a unity." (p. 4) . . . "Communication means a sharing of elements of behavior, or modes of life, by the existence of sets of rules." (p. 6) . . . ". . . communication is not the response itself, but

is essentially the *relationship* set up by the transmission of stimuli and the evocation of responses." (p. 7). Colin Cherry, *On Human Communication*, The M.I.T. Press, Cambridge, Mass., 1966, pp. 4, 6, and 7.

Some people think of communication as occurring only when the people involved create a mutual understanding. The key to communication becomes a responding to each other responding to each other, and each being aware of the other responding to the response of the other. If I recognize you as friend, speak to you as a unique individual who is my friend; you see me and hear me as friend and respond to your seeing and hearing; and I see and hear your response to my responding to seeing you and then hearing you—then we have communicated. Some communicologists think of communication in this way, as a mutual awareness of sharing in a relationship (see Cherry, Insight 1.1, No. 11). If you think of communication in this way, then not all of the situations were answered "yes." The examples of the President on TV and reading this book, probably are *not* communication, by this definition. The rest of the examples *could* be, but we can't tell from the descriptions. Even though messages (verbal and nonverbal) were exchanged in the other examples, there was no indication that sharing (mutual understanding) took place.

There is no "true" or absolutely "right" definition of communication. There are simply different conceptions which have different implications for study and analysis. The way you define and conceive of a communication event determines when you'll use the word "communication" and to what you will refer. (This same general principle applies to all words!) Which conception you choose depends upon your purposes. However, a definition or conception of communication should be established so that we may examine the problems.

DEFINITION OF A COMMUNICATION-STATE

A function of any definition should be to determine when communication occurs and when it does not. The examples in the previous quiz all involve simultaneous message exchanges in the presence of others, but that does not necessarily mean communication has taken place. The issue then becomes: when does communication occur, when does it not occur, and how can its occurrence be differentiated from its non-occurrence? In other words, the issue becomes not what is communication, but what conditions must be met before we can say communication has occurred.

If we accept the definitions of Weaver (No. 2), McCroskey (No. 4), Wenburg and Wilmot (No. 8), or Thayer (No. 9), then communication occurs whenever we interpret or *assign meaning* to the messages of another. In essence, if this type of definition is accepted, then the famous axiom "One *cannot not* communicate" (Watzlawick et al., 1967, p. 51) must also be accepted. This axiom states that people cannot not behave, that behavior will be perceived and interpreted by another, and therefore, a person *cannot not* communicate when he is in another's presence. However pedogogically useful this axiom is, it does not fulfill a major function of a definition—to both exclude as well as include certain things or behaviors. The act of communication becomes a constant in interpersonal exchanges and the discipline lays itself open to Pool's assertion (Thayer, 1967, p. 70) that "any phenomenon that appears as a universal constant in social events should necessarily be of no more than secondary concern to the theorists or researchers."

These assignment-of-meaning definitions appear incomplete in defining when interpersonal communication occurs and when it does not occur. They appear incomplete because they fail to differentiate between situations where human sharing and unity take place and situations where man simply perceives and interprets stimuli from his environment.

Think for a moment about your own experiences with others. Do you feel that every time you talk with another or behave in another's presence (whether you are aware of it or not) that the two of you have communicated? Aren't there times when you feel frustrated and dissatisfied because you know somehow the other person is not with you, that the two of you don't have your act together? If you are a wife, aren't there times you feel you haven't been understood by your husband, even though you know he's heard the words? If you're a student, aren't there times you've aked the question of professors only to hear answers that don't seem at all relevant? You know he heard the words, but you don't feel you've been understood.

If you accept the assignment-of-meaning type of definitions, then you would have to conclude that you have indeed communicated with another person because meaning has been assigned. But no feelings of understanding or satisfaction or acceptance result. Nonetheless, the assignment-of-meaning type of definitions do specify a condition crucial to the identification of the occurrence of communication.

We constantly perceive information from others, which we interpret and evaluate. We provide ourselves with information about another by processing information we receive from the other person. The color and length of hair, the clothes, posture, height, age, word choice and pronunciation, loudness and pitch of the voice are all bits of information we receive from another person. From these bits of information we infer certain things about the person. For example, whether or not he is a student; what part of the country she is from; how he feels about marijuana, she about ecology; whether she is angry, he sad, or she in love. We use any and all of these messages to inform ourselves about what the other person is thinking and doing, whether we want to interact with them, and what they are really like. In other words, the axiom, "One *cannot not* communicate" should read "Any system capable of processing messages *cannot not* inform itself."

Expressed differently, the ability to assign meaning appears to be a necessary condition for the occurrence of communication.* Therefore, in order for communication to occur, the

---

* A *necessary condition* is something that must be present if some other event is to occur. In logical notation, X is a necessary condition for Y, if and only if X precedes every occurrence of Y. For example, excluding artificial insemination techniques, intercourse in humans is a necessary condition for pregnancy, i.e., pregnancy could not occur without it. A *sufficient condition* is something that brings about another event regardless of anything else. In other words, if X, then Y, regardless of what else has occurred. Fertilization is the sufficient condition for pregnancy. It does not matter how the sperm entered the egg, but given fertilization has happened, pregnancy has resulted.

participants must be able to process symbolic information and to assign meaning to messages. However, assigning meaning by itself does not fully explain the emergence of a unity, that is to say the state of communication. If attaching significance to the behavior of others is the necessary condition, what then, is the sufficient condition for creating a communication-state?

Sharing interpretations rather than just receiving information lies at the heart of communication (see Cherry, Insight 1.1, No. 11). Communication, then, is not the mere sending of messages or the assignment of meaning to received messages. Rather, it requires the active response of each participant to the verbal and nonverbal messages given off by the other. Thus, the sufficient condition for creating a communication-state is the mutual realization of understanding—the common recognition by the participants that they are both being understood. When we understand another, we can look at the world from his point-of-view. We see as the other sees and we can accurately predict his meanings for the behavior or situation he sees. On the other hand, the feeling of being understood by another concerns our own ability to know the other is understanding us as we interact. When we realize we are being understood, we become aware that the other views some behavior or situation from our point-of-view. In other words, understanding another refers to our ability to accurately receive information from him, while being understood refers to our ability to know the information we have transmitted has been accurately received. When both persons can accurately predict the other's meanings, and know that their meanings are being accurately received, then a communication-state has been reached.

In summation, a communication-state occurs when two or more persons capable of processing symbolic information and assigning meaning realize that they are understood and understand each other, i.e., realize they have shared meaning.* Unfortunately, you can only guess the amount of mutual understanding needed for a communication-state. The probability of perfect mutual understanding is undoubtedly zero. So, the

---

* See Laing, Phillipson and Lee (1966) and Scheff (1967) for a more rigorous discussion of understanding and being understood.

question of how much mutual understanding is needed becomes crucial in isolating instances of a communication-state and remains one of the empirical questions needing further research.

Several implications naturally follow from our definition. Some of them contradict the belief that telling someone is communicating. All reflect belief in man's humanity and humanness.

A Communication-State Never Can Be Assumed

In interpersonal relations the following kinds of assumptions are typically made:

> First, I assume that I've accurately seen object X; second, I assume that you've accurately seen object X; and third, I assume that you've seen object X in the same way that I've seen object X. (Schutz, 1966)

Different needs, purposes, backgrounds, attention levels, and perceptive abilities can cause any one of these assumptions to be in error. Typically, the third one gets us into the most difficulty in interpersonal relations.

As individuals, we don't communicate with others as often as we'd like to think we do. Just because we talk to another doesn't mean we've reached a communication-state, and just because we exchanged information does not mean we've shared meanings. For instance, in the gas station example the station attendant gave directions which were followed, and the stranger easily arrived at his destination. Proper instructions were given and followed, and the desired goal was reached, but was a unity created? Did the gas station attendant and the traveler realize they'd been understood? From the information given in the example, the answer would have to be "no." There was no mutual recognition of being understood and of understanding. Information was exchanged and interpreted accurately, but, since neither individual *knew* the information was interpreted accurately, no communication-state was created.

Not only didn't the gas station attendant know whether the traveler reached his destination, but he also didn't understand what the destination meant to the traveler. The traveler could have been going to an interview for a job that he wanted very much, or going to pick up a girl friend, or visiting a college friend he hadn't seen in years. Therefore, the gas station attendant didn't understand the traveler's view. On the other hand, the traveler didn't know how the gas station attendant could enjoy helping others; he could be bored with giving directions to out-of-towners; he could see giving directions as part of his job. The traveler did not share meaning with the attendant, he received information from him. The key to developing a communication-state is the responding each does to the other, indicating, "I understand you and you have understood me."

It follows from this discussion that people don't always have to communicate with another (achieve mutual understanding) to accomplish their own goals, to adequately do their jobs, or to get things done. The traveler didn't have to communicate with the gas station attendant to find out how to get to his destination. Likewise, a man doesn't have to communicate with a sales clerk in order to buy toothpaste; a woman doesn't have to communicate with the druggist in order to get her prescription filled; an employee doesn't have to share connotative meanings with his boss in order to adequately perform his job. All that needs to be done in these situations is to have information accurately exchanged between the participants. The sales clerk must be able to get the right brand of toothpaste; the druggist must be able to supply the correct prescription (the woman certainly won't want tranquilizers when she asked for birth-control pills!); the boss doesn't need to understand what the job means to his employee in order to predict employee behavior and adequately coordinate the efforts of the work group. What is needed in these situations is the accurate exchange of information. Interpersonal communication is not necessary (sometimes it is not even desirable, but more will be said of that later).

A Communication-State Is Situation-Bound

The sharing of meanings occurs within a given spatial-temporal setting. The social setting (context) helps us to set expectations about (1) what to perceive, (2) what interpretations for verbal and nonverbal messages are most likely, (3) what relationships are most likely to develop, and (4) how we as individuals are to behave. In other words, whether or not we understand and are understood depends on the particular social setting within which the conversation occurs. This point is so obvious it is easily overlooked, and its importance to the communicative process easily forgotten. For example, if you were in a beer distributor's warehouse, the statement, "This case is heavy!" would mean something different from what it would mean if you were in a lawyer's office. The words are the same, but the situations differ and determine the referent of the symbols. Talking with your professor in his office has different relational implications from talking with him in the coffee shop.

A Communication-State is Content-Bound

Just because two people mutually realize they share meanings on one topic, does not necessarily mean they will mutually understand each other on another. You may be able to understand and be understood by your minister when you're discussing religion, but not when you are discussing foreign policy. You and your date may share meanings when discussing love and marriage, but not when the Alaskan pipeline is the topic of conversation. A husband and wife may understand each other perfectly when working on the family budget, but not when they are discussing how to raise the children. Again, this implication appears obvious, but it is one we often forget when actually conversing with one another.

As individuals we tend to assume that because mutual understanding has taken place before, interpersonal sharing is taking place now. Time has passed, new information has been received, experiences have been lived, and both of us may have new meanings for the issue. Happily though, the more topics on which two people share meanings, the more likely they are to reach a communication-state on a new issue.

A state of communication can be reached only with another interpreter of messages. In the same way that "it takes two to

Tango," it takes two to create a unity. A communication-state emerges from social interaction. This emergence can not take place with a book, a newspaper, or one's self. The sharing of meaning emerges from the mutual transmission and reception of messages. To say that the sharing of meaning emerges, means the reaching of a communication-state can not be pre-planned. This does not mean that certain behaviors can not be considered and planned before you talk with another person (a public speaker needs to carefully plan his message both verbally and nonverbally). Rather, since a communication-state emerges from interaction no planned set of behaviors or series of messages can insure its occurrence.

In other words, the emergence of a communication-state is a mutual activity. You can't do it to me, nor can I do it to you. Instead, a communication-state results from what we do together, or it does not occur at all.

There are a variety of ways of reaching a communication-state, but it can not be obtained by only one person. This is why Rogers' (No. 5) definition of "real communication" as "listening with understanding" isn't complete, either. By this definition, I could communicate with you without you knowing it. "Real communication," then, could be something *I* do, rather than something *we* do and create. Communication could be an individual event, rather than a social event in which individuals participate. Repeating over and over again what you've just said (i.e., "If I've told you once, I've told you a hundred times!") may lead to domination, intimidation, or humiliation of the other, but it probably won't increase the likelihood of reaching mutual understanding.

Given that the state of communication requires at least two persons, the responsibility for achieving this unity is also shared. Realization of a unity is something two persons do together, with both parties responsible for its occurrence or nonoccurrence. Once we begin thinking of communication as unity, we can overcome the myth that "telling is communicating."

Agreement Is Not Necessary To Create
A Communication-State

Agreement with another's point-of-view is neither a necessary nor inevitable result of mutual understanding. In fact, sharing meaning may lead to disagreement, but a disagreement based on mutual understanding, not on unilateral interpretation. "Know thy enemy" is an old saying. From our point-of-view, this statement tells us to understand what makes the other guy tick, so that accurate predictions can be made about what he will do. If you can understand and predict the enemy, then you can anticipate his actions and defend against them or prepare counter-measures for self-protection. Now, we are not saying you should view everyone as your enemy. We use the example to emphasize that agreement is not a necessary result of having shared meanings. The more frequently people reach a communication-state on some topic, the more likely they are to develop the same opinion, but agreement or sameness of opinion is not inevitable as long as other sources of information are available to both parties.

We list this implication last, because it is often the least understood. How many times have you heard people say, "Man, I just can't communicate with him!"? This exclamation doesn't necessarily mean that the people can't or aren't mutually sharing; it may mean that the listener doesn't agree with the speaker. Because the listener disagrees with the speaker's evaluation, the speaker assumes he is not understood and that either they are not communicating, or they cannot communicate.

Have you ever heard a friend say about someone, "If we could just communicate, everything would be all right."? The speaker believes that if the other person would just listen to him, the listener would come to agree with his position.

But, agreement is neither a necessary result of mutually shared meanings nor is it a sufficient indicator that communication has taken place. For instance, two people can agree, that birth-control pills have increased the frequency of non-marital sex, but one may believe that this situation is terrible, while the other may think it's great. Or, two persons can both state that God is dead. However, one believes that religion is becoming less influential, and the other feels that the traditional concept of God is being changed as the church increases in influence. In both examples, the speakers agree with the conclusion, but for entirely different reasons. If those reasons are not explored by the participants then no sharing or mutual recognition of understanding occurs, and no communication takes place.

INSIGHT 1.2   From *On Becoming a Person* by Carl R. Rogers*

I come now to a central learning which has had a great deal of significance for me. I can state this learning as follows: *I have found it of enormous value when I can permit myself to understand another person.* The way in which I worded this statement may seem strange to you. Is it necessary to *permit* oneself to understand another? I think that it is. Our first reaction to most of the statements which we hear from other people is an immediate evaluation, or judgment, rather than an understanding of it. When someone expresses some feeling or attitude or belief, our tendency is, almost immediately, to feel "That's right"; "That's stupid"; "That's abnormal"; "That's unreasonable"; "That's incorrect"; "That's not nice." Very rarely do we permit ourselves to *understand* precisely what the meaning of his statement is to him. I believe this is because understanding is risky. If I let myself really understand another person, I might be changed by that understanding. And we all fear change. So as I say, it is not an easy thing to permit oneself to understand an individual, to enter thoroughly and completely and empathically into his frame of reference. It is also a rare thing.

* Carl R. Rogers, *On Becoming a Person* (Boston: Houghton Mifflin, 1961), p. 18.

To reiterate, agreement is neither a necessary precondition nor result of being in a communication-state. Really getting into another person so that you know him, may highlight the differences between you on a number of topics and issues. Discovery of differences is not something to fear. Actually, our relationship will strengthen as we identify areas of similarity and difference because, once identified, we can deal with them. As we uncover our differences and bring them to light, we are also uncovering the uniqueness of the other—finding out "where he's at." Creating a communication-state between us, then, does not guarantee agreement. Indeed, agreement is an unrealistic goal given the differences between people. But a communication-state will bring a greater awareness of the other person's uniqueness, and with this will come the discovery of our own.

The point is that agreement or disagreement are not sure signs of anything, necessarily. Assuming that communication is always problematic, and error in interpretation is much more frequent than accuracy, *before* stating, "I agree," make sure you know with what you are agreeing or disagreeing.

To review, a state of communication occurs when two or more information-processing units mutually realize they are being understood. The creation of this relational state in a social situation is always problematic, being dependent upon the situation and the content, and does not necessarily require that the participants agree with one another. Again, what is required for communication to emerge is the mutual recognition of understanding—this implies a process, a series of behaviors over time.

EMERGENCE OF A COMMUNICATION-STATE

The emergence of the state of mutual understanding implies a "transactional, symbolic process" (Miller and Steinberg, 1972, p. 43).

Process

To call anything a process is to say that it's *on-going and continual.* The process per se has no inherent beginning or ending, only arbitrary starting and ending points that we, as symbol users, impose upon the stream of activity. For instance, when did your life actually begin? For convenience sake, it is typically stated that your life began when you were born (or was it when you were conceived?). Your life has no inherent beginning, only the one we perceivers impose on it so that you can be recognized and distinguished from other parts of the "booming, buzzing" field of experience. Words, which stop time, create categories from continuous experience. But experience is not static, its processes are all dynamic, continually moving. Much like a photograph, words stop action and give the impression that experience stands still. Nothing could be further from the truth. The world moves on; activity is continual and dynamic.

Another important characteristic of processes is the variables involved *vary concomitantly*. What happens to one variable affects what happens to others. (If there is one thing the field of ecology has emphasized, it is that everything is interconnected; nothing ever happens in isolation; all things are inter-related no matter how indirectly.) This emphasis on the interlocking interdependence of events, rather than on their unilateral effects, is a prime characteristic of a process view of reality. Emphasizing that the development of a communication-state is a process, then, directs our concern to the interpersonal relationship within which people exchange messages. These interpersonal relationships are transactional ones.

**INSIGHT 1.3 From "The Transactionist Assumption,"
by William Pemberton***

Let me discuss now three different ways of talking about an experience; or, I might say, three different assumptions we can make about the nature of reality: the absolutistic, the relativistic, and the transactional. These represent roughly three stages of man's growing sophistication about the nature of himself and his cosmos. They could represent beliefs about reality that we might classify as pre-science, early science, and modern science, respectively. For purposes of demonstration, I sometimes distribute to my lecture groups bits of paper which have been dipped in phenyl-thio-carbamide, a harmless chemical which tastes bitter to approximately seventy percent of the participants, but tasteless to the remaining thirty percent. The papers are prepared by dipping a sheet of typing paper into the solution, drying it, and cutting it up. The result is that each person gets, comparatively speaking, the same amount of the substance. I then make a statement of fact about the event: "There is no taste in the paper," which is valid for me. Then I ask what is the thinking of the group, and get such responses as "You're wrong," "You've a different paper," "You're crazy," "Your taste buds are faulty," and the like. The accumulated scientific information, whether or not you taste the paper, is determined by your inherited genes. The insult patterns started, however, are mostly because of the *assumption* about the event; for instance, one being that if we are having the same experience we must be reacting in the same way "or else someone must be wrong" (or deficient, or what not).

Let us look again at the three different assumptions that predominate man's thinking on this kind of event—whether it is through taste, sight, hearing, or other sensory modalities.

*** The assumption of the "absolutistic" person is that "the taste is in the paper" (i.e., qualities are in things).

*** The assumption of the "relativistic" person is that "the taste is in me" (i.e., qualities are in me; for instance, color is determined by the cones in my eyes); some taste it, some do not, "so who cares?"

*** The assumption of the "transactionist" is that there is a transaction going on between what's in the paper and what's going on in me. Some people react to the transaction in one way, some in another. All I can talk factually about is *my* reaction to the transaction, and then make inferences or inquire about yours.

* William Pemberton, "The Transactionist Assumption," in *Bridges Not Walls*, ed. John Stewart (Reading, Mass.: Addison-Wesley, 1973), pp. 29-30.

Transaction

To say that the development and negotiation of shared meanings is transactional assumes that which meanings are shared depends upon the patterns of mutual influence in a relationship. Asserting the process of reaching a communication-state is transactional expresses a way of looking at experience, a way of knowing. A transactional analysis is concerned primarily with what happens mutually and reciprocally to persons when they interrelate. A transactional viewpoint focuses on the participants as an interdependent unit, on us and what we mutually do with each other.

Rules

"Communication means *sharing* of elements of behavior, or modes of life, by the existence of sets of *rules*," writes Cherry (1966, p. 6). Those rules form guidelines by which we organize ourselves and pattern our interactions. These rules generally refer to "who has the right to define the situation." They are transmitted and observed in the command aspects of the message. For example, my nephew replied "So what" to his mother's statement, "Time for a bath and bed." This "so what" challenged the relational role which permits the mother to define the situation and control her son's behavior. The challenge

21

was responded to immediately! Her "right hand to bottom" response re-established and re-emphasized the relational rule giving mother more control over the son's behavior than he had over hers. A transactional perspective of communicative behavior emphasizes the development of relational rules, how they are maintained and changed through symbolic messages.

INSIGHT 1.4   From *Notes to Myself* by Hugh Prather*

I must do these things in order to communicate: Become aware of you (discover you). Make you aware of me (uncover myself). Be ready to change during our conversation, and be willing to reveal my changes to you.

For communication to have meaning it must have a life. It must transcend "you and me" and become "us." If I truly communicate, I see in you a life that is not me and partake of it. And you see and partake of me. In a small way we then grow out of our old selves and become something new. To have this kind of sharing I cannot enter a conversation clutching myself. I must enter it with loose boundaries, I must give myself to the *relationship*, and be willing to be what grows out of it.

* Hugh Prather, *Notes to Myself* (Moab, Utah: Real People Press, 1970), no pagination.

Symbols

The emergence of the state of communication takes place through the use of symbols. A symbol is something that stands for something else. Words, chemical notations, winks, long hair, algebraic notations are all symbols which have common characteristics. For one thing, symbols are arbitrary. There is no necessary connection between the symbol and the thing it stands for—its referent. The moon is not connected in any way with "moon," this book with "book," or the feeling of love with "love." Any symbol, then, is someone's arbitrary invention. As one of my students likes to say, "Madam Curie could not have named radium wrong." In other words, whatever label she used to distinguish the substance she discovered (radium) from other substances would have been the "right" label, because there is no inherent connection between the invented symbol and its intended referent.

Symbols have no necessary space-time relation to their referent. Symbols can be used anytime and anyplace. The use of the symbol (i.e., word) is not contingent on the presence of the referent. You can use your friend's name anytime and anyplace, whether he is there or not.

A related property of symbols is that their use admits to error. To call a thing a word is to be able to use it incorrectly. Language is inherently uncertain and "for a word to have meaning it must be possible to use it wrongly" (Terwilliger, 1968, p. 158). For instance, when you tell your friend she's mad, she may indeed be mad, or you may be trying to get her angry, or you may interpret what she has done as anger. Just because you state she is mad, does not necessarily mean that she is mad. In other words, because symbols refer to classes of things, they carry multiple interpretations across situations and within any given situation. Given that symbol-users have multiple interpretations for the same symbol, error is not only possible, but inevitable, and is always present in interpersonal transactions.

But, if symbols are arbitrarily assigned, have no necessary connection with their referent, and are error-prone, how can we talk with others? Symbols are useful because some group of individuals has agreed on their usage. Language is a tremendously useful tool, and its usefulness depends on the extent to which consensus has been reached about how symbols will be used. People in a society or organization can accurately exchange information and communicate because they have agreed on the usages of their commonly-shared symbols. Standardized usages for specific symbols are developed by a group within a particular situation when a given symbol has one, and only one, referent. For instance, I used to work for a company that made recreational vehicles. My first day on the job, I was told to get some corner, eight feet of flat and ten feet of cove. "Riiigght," I replied. The words "corner," "flat," and "cove" refer to types of wood trim used to decorate the inside of trailers. Within that factory, those symbols had very precise referents and conveyed accurate information among the company's employees. Every

23

social unit—whether a married pair, a group, an organization, a society—develops these standardized usages for symbols within a specific social situation. Their use decreases the number of possible interpretations for the symbol, decreases the probability of error, and increases the probability of accurately exchanging information. But these usages are precise only within a given situation and among a given group of persons.

If an individual does not know the standardized usage within that particular context, he becomes confused and disoriented. This is why many persons have experienced fluent knowledge of a foreign language in the classroom, but then feel mute when placed in the culture that actually uses that language. This learning of language usage is also part of "learning the ropes" within an organization. Of course, the larger the group, the greater the probability that lack of consensus and error will result, so that information will not be accurately transmitted and misunderstandings will result.

Furthermore, symbolic messages have at least two levels of meaning, called the *report* and *command* aspects of messages. The report aspect concerns the referent of the symbols. The command aspects are relational, suggesting who has the right to control the situation. For instance, your roommate asks you in a pleasant voice to "close the window." Since only one window in the room is open, you clearly know which window is being referred to—the report aspect. But also contained in this message is the implication that the speaker has the right to make this request, that he has the right to control your actions in this way—the command aspect. If you believe that the request is legitimate, i.e., believe the other can control you in this way, then you will probably close the window. If not, then you might respond by saying curtly "Close it yourself."

Another example would be the young man who asks his date up to his apartment to hear his new record album. The young lady easily identifies the report aspects of the message, but her response is determined by how she assesses the command aspects of his words. Is the guy implying a friendship relation where they will share some time together listening to music, or is he implying a sexual encounter which he may or may not have the right to initiate? What are his intentions? What type of relationship is he suggesting? Let's assume that the guy intended a friendship relation, while the girl assumed he intended a "less honorable" relationship. What happens when the guy and the girl get up to his apartment and no advances are made? The girl may interpret the lack of moves as meaning the guy doesn't like her, that she is not attractive and/or that the guy is shy and withdrawn and will probably be dull company. The guy, on the other hand, sensing that something has changed, may interpret her coolness as meaning she doesn't like him and/or, she is nervous about being in his apartment, and therefore, he shouldn't try anything. He decides to be extremely polite to assure her his intentions are "honorable." The evening progresses along awkwardly and ends with both persons thinking he/she was not liked, and they will probably not have another date. What happened? The referential or report aspects of the messages were clear enough, but because the command or relational definitions were not shared, no understanding developed and a communication-state did not result.

Because of the many differences in experiences and attitudes, referential meanings are hard enough to share, and relational aspects are even more difficult to negotiate and understand. Yet, understanding at the relational level is crucial if a communication-state is to emerge in interpersonal conversations.

WAYS TO OVERCOME THE MYTH

1. Stop thinking of communication as telling—as the act of speaking to others. Until the belief "telling equals communication" is removed, further advances toward the development of a communication-state are difficult.

2. Develop an awareness of error—the awareness that error is an inherent part of human interaction, the awareness that we cannot eliminate error, but we can minimize its effect.

a. As people speak to you, ask them questions. Questions encourage others to give you more information about what they are saying. They feel important because you are asking. You get more information about their frame-of-reference so you can interpret their messages to you with greater accuracy (closer to the position they intended).

b. When people ask you questions about what you mean, answer them. Often we take questions as insults to our ability to use language. Such thinking forgets that communication is situation-bound and content-bound, a transactional process using symbols, involving people who are different. A question doesn't say, "you're stupid." Rather, a question says "I don't understand your message and through your message, you. I want to understand. Please, tell me more."

c. Expect the development of a communication-state to take time. "Getting into" another person will be a slow process. You will need to interact in different social situations often before each can predict the thoughts, feelings, and actions of the other accurately enough to be understanding and understood. It's easier to say than to do, but be patient—a relationship is trying to bloom.

3. Practice the sending of messages carefully designed to be specific and accurate.

a. Create a speech in which your objective is to let your listeners "know" an important part of you. For example, create a speech on some attitude or belief you hold, describing why you hold it, and how the belief affects your life, your everyday speaking with others. Carefully select the language you will use in the speech. Perhaps you will need to write a manuscript in order to be sure what you want to say will be said exactly as you wish to say it. Give the speech to a friend. Ask him to interrupt you whenever he "doesn't understand." Occasionally, stop and ask him to tell you in his own words what you have been saying.

b. Create a speech in which your objective is to inform your listeners on some technical topic; i.e., the law of supply and demand, the modulations in television frequencies, sculpting with metals. Carefully divide the topic into small units, each unit describing some aspect of the topic. Carefully select specific colorful language designed to stimulate vivid mental images of the minds of the listeners—let them "see" in their mind's eye what you are talking about. Maybe you will have to write-out a manuscript to choose and arrange the language. Present the speech to a friend. Ask him to stop you anytime he feels unsure about what you are saying. Stop and ask him to tell you in his own words what you have been saying.

4. Create a small group of from 5 – 7 people. Talk enough to find some topic that is controversial (i.e., abortion or pre- and extramarital sex). Begin to discuss the topic with the objective of exploring your different points-of-view. One rule: no one may speak until the preceding speaker's remarks have been paraphrased. This is difficult and frustrating. Difficult, because we don't often listen carefully, and frustrating, because the repetition slows the discussion. But your objective is not to resolve your differences, but to explore them: to find out what the other people think and feel and why. If you have enough time and everyone in the group is willing to put forth the energy, your group could create a communication-state. If everyone's view can be understood by the group and the group members can be understanding of each other, then that rare period of mutual sharing can develop. You won't all agree on the topic but you will have improved your understanding of the various views. Discovering your differences and similarities will lead you into discovering the uniqueness of the others.

SUMMARY

There seems to be a belief in our society, a myth, which says that communicating is telling—the sending of messages to one another. Believing the myth often prevents us from making contact with others. After looking at interpersonal conversations and theoretical definitions, we've inferred that all of us want to achieve the state of mutual understanding when we talk together; therefore, we have to think of communication as mutual understanding. Individuals reach a communication-state when they both know that they are understanding and are being understood. Developing that understanding requires a thorough awareness of the complexities of the communication process.

27

A communication-state can not be assumed to have occurred; indeed, errors and misunderstandings are inherent in the process. The process takes place within social situations which potently affect the means and manner in which we speak with one another. Making contact is affected also by the content of the messages sent. Further, achieving a communication-state requires us—it is a mutual activity, demanding that both people assume responsibility. We have also seen that people don't have to agree with one another in order to communicate. Examining the process of sharing meaning, we have found it to be continuous, transactional, symbolic and characterized by rules governing the behaviors of the participants. Finally, suggestions have been given to help all of us to overcome the myth.

Since meaning and understanding are so important to communication, we need to turn our attention now to meaning within interaction.

2

THE MEANING
OF MEANING

MYTH

*"If You Don't Know What
the Word Means, Look It Up!"*

A friend of mine recently called his girl at work to ask about having lunch together. He suggested that they meet at a place called Knapp's. She agreed and said she'd be there at 12:15. Now, in this particular city, there is a department store named Knapp's which houses a restaurant, and there is a Bill Knapp's restaurant, often referred to as simply Knapp's. She went to the department store; he went to the restaurant. Needless to say, they did not meet for lunch. Later that afternoon, he called her back, and the following conversation took place:

He: "Where were you? I waited as long as I could, but ... at least you could have called to say ...."

She: (interrupting) "What do you mean, where was I? Where were you? Standing me up for lunch! I'd gotten us a booth, and I sat there all alone, with your unused water glass staring me in the face, reminding me how inconsiderate you are."

He: (getting mad) "Wait a darned minute! I was there at exactly 12:15. Looked for you and then sat down to read the paper in the waiting area just inside the door. You never showed. So I grabbed a quick sandwich and left about 12:45."

She: (challenging his statement) "You couldn't have been. I got there . . ."

He: (interrupting and getting angrier) "Don't tell me I couldn't have been. I was there at exactly the time . . ."

She: "What waiting area? Knapp's doesn't have a waiting area where you could sit down and read the paper."

He: "What? It sure does. Just inside the door, you walk into a built-in seat that's about 20 feet long. I sat right there and . . ."

She: "No, it doesn't. Bill Knapp's has that kind of waiting area, but Knapp's doesn't."

He: "What are you talking about? Bill Knapp's *is* Knapp's —the place where you were to meet me for lunch, remember?"

She: (now knowing where the mistake was made, sweetly) "No, it isn't dear. The department store Knapp's also has a restaurant. That's where I was—at Knapp's, just like you said."

He: (apologetically) "I'm sorry, honey. What I meant was Bill Knapp's . . ."

In this example each assumed that words have meanings, that somehow words magically convey an idea or thought to the listener. If one can hear, one will understand instantly what is said. The couple, by not defining exactly which Knapp's, assumed their luncheon arrangements set. They knew what the words meant; there was no need "to look it up." But, what the words meant to the listener was not what was inteded by the speaker.

MEANINGS ARE IN PEOPLE

If communicologists can make one definitive statement, it is that meanings are not in words. Words in and of themselves do not mean anything. Words are simply tools by which we can describe differences in our environment, distinguish different objects, persons, and events in our surroundings. Notice that as we use words to refer to differences in our surroundings, to label our environment, we actually create our reality out of the words (symbols). Therefore, each of us lives in a symbolic world which we have created and to which we assign meaning.

As individuals, we create the only reality we will ever know. Although these acts of creation heighten our sense of individuality and uniqueness, it is not "a cause for unqualified celebration. It turns out, for example that John Donne was wrong. Each man *is* an island entire to himself" (Postman and Weingartner, 1969, p. 99). Experiences, needs, purposes, assumptions, and, therefore, perceptions and meanings are unique to the individual. It follows from this notion that no one can be absolutely certain of anything. You can not "tell it like it is"; the best you can do is tell how you perceive it and what it means to you. There are no absolutely correct perceptions and meanings provided by our environment waiting to be discovered. The concept of relativity and the uncertainty principle are much more than the jargon of the physicist: they are basic perceptual principles that each of us lives every second of our life.

However, some persons tend to assume that there is an absolutely correct interpretation of events, and it is up to the individual to discover the "right" one. After these correct interpretations are discovered, they are then labelled with some word. This word, then, is thought to carry the correct meaning to anyone capable of hearing and processing. This assumption is humorously but often sadly observed in our everyday talking in the "I Told Them So Fallacy" (Berlo, 1960, pp. 176–177). Think for a moment about the number of times you've heard someone (like a boss, mother, brother, friend) say something like:

"I just don't understand what went wrong. I told them what to do. If I told them once, I told them a hundred times! They just don't listen."

Whenever you hear a phrase like this, you can be sure that the speaker has assumed that words have meanings, and that communication is nothing more than dumping the "right" words on the listener.

31

An unfortunate but typical result of believing this fallacy is that hard feelings and negative judgments are made about the listener: madness ("That guy is nuts!") and/or badness ("That guy is lazy, dumb and just doesn't give a damn!"). The speaker, on the other hand, will often be judged as unfair ("What does he expect of me, anyway?"), unclear ("Well, if you'd have just said *that,* I'd have known."), or unable to give instructions ("He may be bright and competent, but he sure can't get his point across."). A defensive spiral may be initiated whereby each person tries—often by shouting—to defend himself from the other's verbal attack.

Some of you may be saying, "But certainly, words have meanings. After all, isn't that what the dictionary is for?" Dictionaries, however, describe referential uses of words. Dictionaries do not prescribe how the words should be used. The 500 most common words in the English language have over 14,000 definitions listed in the dictionary—that is just about 28 "meanings" per word. When you hear one of these words, how do you know which one of the 28 is meant? If you "know" at all (Bill Knapp's was not Knapp's), the meaning you know is based on your previous experience and the social context within which the message was transmitted.

GIVING MEANING TO MEANING

Perhaps it is time to state what we mean by "meaning." In terms of the interpersonal focus considered here, "meaning" emerges in conversation when words (symbols) are placed in a relational framework that makes the behavior, thought, or feeling mentioned, understandable to the listener. "Meaning," then, is more than just recognizing the referent of some symbol or set of symbols. Meaning involves placing those symbols in a relational framework, making the information functional, understandable, or self-evident to the other.

As we have said, in order to interrelate, people must know what is being referred to (the "report" aspect of a message) as well as how the referent is being discussed in terms of the situation and the relationship between the interactants (the

32

"command" aspect of the message). In other words, to assign meaning to a particular message, each of us makes judgments about the referent of the symbols and about the speaker's intentions (toward the referent and the listener). The assignment of meaning to a symbolic message, then, is situationally bound and involves an interpretation of the other's intentions.

Remember, we stated earlier that being able to process information is the necessary condition for creating a state of communication, while the realization of shared meanings is its sufficient condition. Let's see how necessary and sufficient conditions relate to shared meanings.

Let's suppose that you and a friend are walking out of class and overhear one of your male professors ask a female student out for a drink. What does that mean? Specifically, you heard the instructor say, "I'll meet you at The Friendly at 4 o'clock, okay, Sherry?" The referents in this message are the professor, the bar (The Friendly), and Sherry, the female student. Assuming that you and your friend know all these places and persons, the two of you can quickly agree on the referents for the symbols (words) used in the sentence you've overheard. But the question still remains, what does it mean? The message could mean the professor wants to date Sherry and has strictly non-professional intentions. His statement could mean also that the girl wants to talk to her instructor about an academic problem, and the professor has suggested a less formal atmosphere than his office. Or, the message could mean that the instructor and the girl are simply good friends and enjoy talking to each other informally. Which interpretation you pick will determine what the overheard statement means to you, since each interpretation implies a different relationship. The first implies a lover-type relationship; the second maintains a professional student-teacher relationship; the third implies a friend-type relationship. No matter which interpretation you choose, the behavior (professor meeting female student for a drink) becomes understandable to you. By guessing the professor's intentions and putting the overheard message into a relational framework, you have assigned meaning to his behavior (the necessary condition for communication). As soon as you and your friend realize that each of you has the same interpretation of the professor's behavior (the sufficient condition), then you and your friend have communicated. Which interpretation you choose is, of course, affected by such things as (a) your perception of the girl and of the professor; (b) the way in which the professor said his words, the way he looked, i.e., his nonverbal behavior; (c) the way the girl looked at the professor, i.e., her nonverbal behavior; (d) your own perceptions of all professors and all girls; (e) your own self-concept.

Each of these variables will be discussed later. In the next few pages, let's look at the implications of our "meaning" definition and how one comes to assign meanings to symbolic behavior.

Meanings For Symbols Are Social In Origin

Man is a social animal. Men are interdependent, and each man learns about himself and his environment through interaction with others. A large proportion of this interaction is carried on through the use of symbols (words). The words we use take their meanings from what we have experienced in particular social situations. For example, if you were raised in a white community where blacks were believed to be inferior, chances are you now believe blacks are inferior to whites. Your meaning for the symbol "blacks" developed through your interactions with others in your social environment. Or, if you have played the game of football, the symbol "football" has a meaning for you different from that of a person who has not played the game. If you are now married, the symbol "marriage" has meanings different from the ones it had prior to your wedding day. That meanings are learned through experience is so obvious as to apear trivial, but how many of us remember it when speaking with others?

Since meanings are learned, they result from our relationships with objects and persons in our environment. "Meanings are in people" in the sense that people act and meanings emerge from one's relationships with others and/or objects. Meanings are not inherent in me, they result from my behaviors with some object or person.

What we are suggesting is that symbols take on meanings as

one learns to deal with and understands how to behave with an object and/or person. The symbol "chair" has meaning because we know what to do with it (i.e., it's a place to rest. The word "student" has meaning because you know you are to behave passively and accept the wisdom that pours from the teacher's mouth. But, if we change our behavior (the manner in which we relate) toward the object or person, the meaning of the symbol changes. Sometimes a chair may be used as a step-ladder; a student may want to actively learn rather than passively receive and regurgitate information. Each one of these meanings implies a different relationship with the object or person, and hence, different ways of behaving with and toward that object or person.

We've been exemplifying differences in referential meaning. Also, each of us has our own idiosyncratic and connotative meanings for words, phrases, events, and situations. Connotative meanings (the emotional dimension of meaning) are unique to us. Yet, as people trying to make contact with others, we must talk in words that are not unique to us, but are common to a given group of language users. This presents a problem. How can you make contact with my world and share my own private symbolic reality so that you know what *I* mean, when you use common words which have typical referents? By negotiating with me the meanings the two of us will have for the words—the meanings we will share.

Meanings change as people change.

If meanings are the result of your relationships with other objects and persons, and if you encounter new objects and persons or familiar objects and persons in new situations, then your meaning (your referential and relational interpretations) will change over time and situations. For instance, it is hoped that your meaning for communication will be changed after you read this book. As you go through college, your interpretation of what is "means" to be a student will slowly but surely change over time (see Insight 2.1).

Likewise, your interpretations of marriage, of parenthood, of work, of love, etc., will all slowly change over time. A friend of mine told me that she was truly amazed at the way in which her love for her husband had grown since they'd been married. She had thought when she got married that her love was at its peak, that she could not love him any more than she did at the time. But, as she experienced him in new ways and in new settings, her love and respect for her husband continued to grow. In her own words, the relationship she'd had with him before they were married was almost "trite and shallow" compared to what it is now.

INSIGHT 2.1   Changes in College Students' Attitudes and Excuses Over Time

	FRESHMAN	SOPHOMORE	JUNIOR	SENIOR
AMBITION	To be graduated with a 4.0 and get a high-paying job	To be graduated with a 3.0 and get a decent job	To be graduated	To avoid welfare
PROFESSORS	They know everything	They know something	They don't know much	They don't know shit
TARDINESS	I didn't leave the dorm in time	I missed the bus	The bus was late	The - - - - - bell rang early

---

The poem "Remember" in Insight 2.2 is a good illustration of: (1) the flexibility of language, (2) the multiple interpretations of symbols, depending upon grammatical and social context, and (3) the way in which words are used, changing their "meanings" over time. (P.S. If the author believes that "English it's NOT," then she believes the myth.)

Forgetting that people and situations change over time may be fun and entertaining at times, but it can have tragic results, also. For instance, have you visited an old friend or relative and talked and behaved the way you used to with him, though you, yourself, no longer act this way? You and your friend have both individually changed, but your perceptions of each other and of your relationship are based on the behaviors, opinions, and ideas the two of you used to share. So, when the two of you get together and re-new old times, you are literally re-experiencing what you were *then*, not what you are *now*. This is often fun and entertaining, like at conventions, high school and college reunions, family holidays, etc. But, disregarding and/or not allowing for changes may be frustrating, embarrassing, and is potentially painful. For example, when your parents refuse to "see" you as an adult and continually re-assert their right to prescribe and control your behavior; when people "see" a criminal after the guy has served his time and "gone straight"; when people "see" an alcoholic who hasn't had a drink in years; when . . . The point is, you *can not assume* that what meanings were accurate yesterday are necessarily valid today.

INSIGHT 2.2   "Remember" Indiana University Publications*

Remember when HIPPIE meant big in the hips,
And a TRIP involved travel in cars, planes, and ships?
When POT was a vessel for cooking things in,
And HOOKED was what Grandmother's rug might have been.
When FIX was a verb that meant mend or repair,
And BE IN meant simply existing somewhere.
When NEAT meant well organized, tidy and clean.
And GRASS was a ground cover, normally green.
When lights and not people were SWITCHED ON and OFF.
And the PILL might have been what you took for a cough.

When CAMP meant to quarter outdoors in a tent,
and POP was what the weasel went?
When GROOVY meant furrowed with channels and hollows,
and BIRDS were winged creatures, like robins and swallows.
When FUZZ was a substance that's fluffy like lint
and BREAD came from bakeries, not from the mint?
When SQUARE meant a 90-degree angled form,
and COOL was a temperature not quite warm.
When ROLL meant a bun, and ROCK was a stone.
And HANG-UP was something you did to a phone?

37

When CHICKEN meant poultry, and BAG meant a sack?
And JUNK trashy cast-offs and old bric-a-brac.
When CAT was a feline, a kitten grown up,
When TEA was a liquid you drank from a cup?
When SWINGER was someone who swung in a swing, and a PAD
    was a soft sort of cushiony thing?
When WAY OUT meant distant and far, far away,
And a man couldn't sue you for calling him GAY?
When DIG meant to shovel and spade in the dirt,
And PUT-ON was what you would do with a shirt.

When TOUGH described meat too unyielding to chew,
And MAKING A SCENE was a rude thing to do?
Words once so sensible, sober and serious
Are making the FREAK SCENE like PSYCHEDELIRIOUS.
It's GROOVY, MAN, GROOVY, but English it's not.
Methinks that the language has gone straight to POT.

* Anonymous Author

The world is rapidly and continually changing. Events hurry by us; knowledge is doubling about every five years; you are doing things today that few thought possible just a few years ago. The world is not static or stagnant, neither must be your meanings for those events. So, if you want to understand and be understood by someone, check your assumptions about him. You will often find that he is not the person you thought he was, and often, to your amazement, you may not be the person you thought you were.

No Two People Have Exactly The Same Meaning For The Same Symbol

If meanings are learned through experience, then no two people will have exactly the same meanings for the same symbol. Why? No two people can ever have exactly the same set of experiences. Even if we learn common referential meanings, the connotative aspects of meaning assignment (the emotions we attach to the symbols) will vary with each individual's emotional experiences. However, if two people have had similar experiences and acquired similar information about some event, they are more likely to have similar meanings. Further, since a communication-state results when meanings are shared, the more similar the experiences people have had, the more likely they are to share, to mutually realize they understand and are understood.

Ask yourself for a moment, how likely is it that a person raised in the suburbs can understand what it "means" to live in a ghetto? How likely is it that an individual who has not experienced the Great Depression will understand what it "means" to be without even the most basic necessities? (See Insight 2.3.) How likely is it that a person who has never smelled and/or tasted the horror of war will understand what it "means" to suffer constantly the fear of death? How likely is it that a person who has never been loved can understand what it "means" to love.

INSIGHT 2.3   From *The Pursuit of Loneliness* by Philip E. Slater*

In the recent past, . . . and in the working-class families today, parents sacrificed in order to prepare their children to be economically and socially better off than the parents were, and often hated them for fulfilling this goal and leaving the parents behind. Now middle-class parents sacrifice in order to prepare their children to be emotionally better off—more loving, expressive, creative, cooperative, honest—and once again, resent being outdistanced. In both cases the parents feel left out of the triumphs they made possible; and the children feel ashamed of the parents who wanted them to be superior. The parents want their fantasies of vicarious success fulfilled but never seem to recognize that both kinds of success involve a change to a new milieu from which the parents are automatically excluded. The earlier group of parents wanted their children to become rich and respectable and still remain somehow part of the working class milieu. The later group want their children to be more cultured, less money-grubbing, more spontaneous and creative, yet somehow willing to remain on the same treadmill with the parents.

* Philip E. Slater, *The Pursuit of Loneliness* (Boston: Beacon Press, 1970), p. 77.

However, human difference has been called the "prime obstacle to every form of communication" (Haney, 1967). The inability to have similar experiences and relationships forms part of the rationale contending there will always be gaps separating people: only Indians can understand the Indian experience; only other handicapped people can understand being blind; a man cannot "really" understand what it's like to be a woman. There is no question that a young man today cannot understand the spirit of sacrifice and concern for material security that emerged from the Depression; a W.A.S.P. cannot "really" know what it's like to be a minority; a man cannot "really" experience the ambivalence of menstruation, pregnancy, and childbirth. These differences are genuine and make a difference in the way one perceives and interprets the environment. The crucial question is not whether these observable differences make individuals different, but rather how much of a difference they make in people's ability to share meanings and communicate. The myths about words and meanings manifested in the "I told you . . ." and "Look it up . . ." statements assume meanings are static because (the assumption goes) the meanings rest in the words and not in the people.

FRAME OF REFERENCE

Each of us can perceive events and respond to symbols only in terms of our own "frame of reference" (our individual and uniquely organized set of symbols). The idea of frame of reference as an important concept in the communication process is based on the following four propositions (originally stated by Carl Rogers).*

(1) Each person lives in a constantly changing world of which he is the center. People and events are not static, but dynamic. They interact and are interdependent. What happens to one person affects, however slightly and indirectly, what is

---

* The following is based on Haney's (1967, pp. 63–65) paraphrasing of C. Rogers in *Client-Oriented Therapy*, pp. 483–494.

happening or will happen to another. Stating that we live in a continually changing world asserts a *process* view of reality.

(2) Each person reacts to and acts in his world as he experiences and perceives it; thus, one's perceptual world is "reality." The perceptual process is primarily one of categorization (Bruner, 1958). A person's category system depends on his symbolic milieu (the kinds of symbols an individual uses to recognize, recode, and remember differences in his environment). Each of us perceives and thinks according to his own set of symbols. Therefore, we live in a world that is a function of our symbolic system. We don't directly "see" the people, things, events around us. Rather, we symbolically categorize what our senses receive (perception) and then assign meaning to these perceptual categories. What is out there in "reality" isn't anything at all until we classify it, and then "it" is whatever we've made it. The view that reality is a function of one's language system has sometimes been called the "Sapir-Whorf Hypothesis." These two anthropologists were particularly interested in the effects of different language systems. They concluded that every language represents a unique way of classifying and perceiving the environment and that every language-user resides in the house built by his symbolic categories.

To the extent that any two or more persons share common symbols, category systems, and categorization processes, the probability of constructive interaction and mutually satisfying communication increases. To the extent that any two or more persons' symbols, categories, and categorization processes are unique and idiosyncratic, the likelihood of mutual understanding and mutual goal attainment decreases. This is so, even though individualistic perceptual groupings may simultaneously increase one's creative and imaginative abilities.

(3) Each individual strives to actualize, maintain, and enhance his own self-concept. A person's self-concept, the way one perceives oneself, both affects and is affected by one's perceptions of his surroundings. Furthermore, it follows from earlier analysis that one's self-concept, like all perceptual categories, is a function of one's symbolic system. In the same way that a person's symbolic system shapes his "reality," it simultaneously shapes his "self-concept," so that "reality" and "self"

are both encapsulated within one's set of symbols; i.e., both are symbolic.

(4) The best way to understand and communicate with another is in terms of *his symbolic system,* his organized, subjective frame of reference. However, complete understanding of another's frame of reference would be impossible, since we all have had different experiences. Therefore, the best we can do at any given time is to guess, estimate, or predict what another's frame of reference looks like and includes. In order to be accurate in our predictions and understandings of another, we have to get out of our own frame of reference and get into his. But this, too, is impossible, because *we are our frame of reference*—that uniquely organized set of symbols. In other words, probably the single greatest deterrent to understanding another (to accurately perceiving his subjective reality) is the difference between us—our own internal frame of reference, our own idiosyncratic, subjective, symbolic reality. For meanings to be shared, we both must get out of our own symbolic reality and into the other's. We must continually negotiate what the symbols mean to each of us, referentially and relationally. The most frequently attempted way of establishing this unity is through the use of some language system.

Words are a primary means of relating. They are tools by which and through which we establish our interpersonal relationships. Like any tool, they can be used wisely and carefully, or foolishly and haphazardly. Unlike other tools, however, their effects are less easily predicted and observed. Be careful how you use these tools, since the relationships you build may not be the ones you intend.

WAYS TO OVERCOME THE MYTH

Our conversational abilities, and hence, our chances of reaching communication-states can be improved, although no set of instructions can guarantee that meanings will be shared. The following suggestions are listed for improving our verbal skills, but please remember, we are both speaker and listener simultaneously.

The Speaker's Responsibility

1. Make the message complete. When talking about some idea, experience, feeling or perception, give the listener enough information to know where you're coming from. Enough background information should be presented to allow the listener to get into your frame of reference. However, too much or too detailed information, or statistics, should be avoided because these might bore, intimidate or overwhelm the listener.

2. Talk in the language of the listener. Use words, phrases, slang, and/or jargon you can reasonably expect the listener to understand, both in terms of your reference and your connotation. Why? Because their use implies a concern for the listener's point-of-view and conveys an honest attempt to be understood. Talking in the language of the other implies that the speaker wants to be understood, is involved with the other person, and is committed to establishing a communication-state. Big words, fancy phrases, or specific group slang may sound impressive, but they rarely help create understanding. (Of course, if you want to impress or dominate the other, rather than be understood, big words, fancy phrases, or obscure slang will surely assist you in the effort.)

3. Increase the redundancy of your messages. Say the same thing in a variety of ways. Don't just repeat previously misunderstood phrases (i.e., "If I've told you once, I've . . ."), but restate your idea in different words. If you're giving a speech or a report, use graphs, charts, films, slides, and/or mimeos to help the listener understand the information being presented. There is an old speech instructor's adage which states that the speaker, in organizing his speech, should (a) tell them what he's going to say, (b) tell them, and (c) tell them what he told them. This is good advice.

4. Be consistent in your verbal and nonverbal messages. According to Mehrabian (1968), about 93 percent of the emotional impact of the message is provided nonverbally. If your vocal cues, body movements, dress and appearance seem to contradict the words you express, the nonverbal cues, and not the words, will be used by the listener to determine your intended message. Several common examples come readily to

mind: the professor who glances at his watch and drums his fingers while stating how concerned he is about your problem with writing your paper; the husband who yawningly affirms, "Of course I love you, dear"; the woman who screams, "I'm not upset!"; the professor who looks like he's just finished modeling for *Gentleman's Quarterly* saying, "This is going to be an informal class." Somehow, the listener just can't believe the words. The listener uses the nonverbal messages to establish the intention of the message.

5. The speaker should clearly and unambiguously take responsibility for the ideas, information, thoughts, and opinions expressed in his message. The thoughts expressed are his, not some ill-defined and/or unidentifiable "they" or "everybody knows . . ." or "all people believe . . ." By assuming responsibility for the information presented, the speaker helps to reveal himself to the listener. The listener, then, is in a better position to assess the speaker's intentions and what the implied relationship between them is. By clearly and unambiguously accepting responsibility for the message, a certain amount of involvement with and respect and trust for the other person is implied.

6. Encourage questions. Remember that communication cannot be assumed. Start with the assumption that misunderstanding is likely, then try to get the listener involved in your frame of reference. Periodically, ask what the listener believes, feels, and thinks about what's been said. Try not to ask, as we all tend to do, "Do you understand?" That encourages a "yes" response. Rather, ask, "What do you understand?" Then allow the other person to express his interpretations and connotations of the message presented. Giving a monologue may strengthen your own vocal cords and/or ego, but may encourage the other person to withdraw. Encourage the listener to actively participate in your world—to ask questions is to encourage such participation.

The Listener's Responsibility

1. Listen and question in order to discover the frame of reference of the speaker. The speaker may state complete messages, talk in the listener's language, take responsibility for the

information transmitted, be constructively redundant, present a consistent image and encourage questions and involvement; but, the listener determines whether or not a state of communication will emerge. A good listener can salvage a poor speaker much more effectively than a good speaker can salvage a bad listener. We don't like to hear this because listening is hard work. It takes time, energy, and an emotional commitment to get involved with the other person. Our schools heavily emphasize the transmission (writing and speaking) and not the reception (listening) of messages. Much more will be said about listening in chapter 3, but suffice it to say here that *the goal of listening is to understand*. When receiving messages, the first goal should be understanding the other; then evaluating, analyzing, or criticizing what's been said.

2. Listening requires that we (a) be open and flexible, and try to become a participant in the world of the other person, and (b) demonstrate in some way that we've understood the message sent by the other person.

SUMMARY

There seems to be a myth held by our society that meaning is found in words. So, to find out what words mean we should "look them up" in the dictionary. Believing this myth prevents us from realizing why symbolic messages are often misunderstood.

In exposing the fallacy of this myth, we have said that people create meanings, that meanings emerge from interpersonal conversations. As such, the meaning any given word generates within an individual is referential, is affected by that individual's emotional connotations, and has varying relational implications. Furthermore, meanings are learned within a social context, and change over time. Given these characteristics of meaning-assignment, we can assume that meanings for the same symbol will differ between people. Therefore, to "look it up" may give us a range of acceptable uses, but will not tell us what the other individual meant—maybe not referentially, probably not relationally, and certainly not connotatively. We "see" the world from our own frame of reference. What meaning is

45

assigned to that world is dependent upon the symbols available to us. Finally, we have given suggestions to help overcome the myth of meaning.

But, speaking words requires someone to listen and respond. To these communication skills and responsibilities, we now turn our attention.

3

LISTENING AND FEEDBACK

MYTH
"I Hear You!
I'm Listening!"

INSIGHT 3.1   What You Heard

I
Know That
You Believe You
Understand What You
Think I Said, But I Am Not
Sure You Realize That What You Heard
IS NOT WHAT I MEANT

While in graduate school, my wife and I were visited by a number of sales people. One particular fellow was selling encyclopedias. We let him in because we were interested in purchasing a set. He laid out his samples and visual materials with great care, pointing to important information on each chart and poster. Soon, our small living room was cluttered with his materials. Then, he played a cassette tape recording of the "sales manager" who gave a verbal pitch to buy. (It turned us off because of the depersonalized method.) Next, we discussed the materials, the recording and several of the advantages of owning this particular encyclopedia—yearly updating and research service. "What do you do?" he asked. "I teach speech . . . some classes deal with helping people relate to others; some deal with how to give a public speech." Later, when it looked to him as if we weren't going to buy, the salesman reminded us that we "could have our speeches written for us free of charge with the bonus coupons" we would receive for purchasing his set. It was then that we threw him out! To suggest that a teacher of speech needed someone else to write his speeches for him was the final insult that guaranteed him the loss of the sale. The salesman probably heard my occupation, but he didn't listen.

Several years ago, while still a debate coach who traveled widely, I had the following experience. The squad was preparing for a series of tournaments involving virtually all 30 debaters and the entire coaching staff of five. Several of the events would be qualification for still other, more important tournaments, i.e., the national championships for both the experienced and the novice debaters. One particularly harassing afternoon, a girl we didn't know lingered around my office door. She paced and peered in every once in a while. I ignored her. Finally, I left the office, heading for a practice debate, and she stopped me. "May I see you for a few minutes?" she asked in a whine. "I'm very busy today. How about tomorrow during my office hours, 11 to noon," I flipped off as I walked past her to the practice session. The next day she came back. After the beginning formalities, the who, I found out the why of the visit. She was a freshman, Catholic, living in a house with several guys and two other girls, pregnant and infected with syphilis. The day before, her doctor had confirmed the pregnancy and the VD. My office was the first door she had found open as she wandered around the campus after leaving the doctor's office. She needed someone to talk to about her problem—the fear, hatred, love, concern for parents, and confusion she was feeling. And what had I done? I had told her to "come back tomorrow" during my office hours! I had heard her, but I hadn't been listening. If I had been listening, she would have received help when she needed it. By the way, once I got over my initial embarrassment about my own behavior and shook off my concern for my own stupidity, we got on to the girl's problems and their solutions. Eventually, she got herself together.

LISTENING DESCRIBED

One myth we tend to believe is that listening occurs when we hear another's words. But, listening is more than the mere reception of sound: it is the most important communication skill needed for human interaction, both in interpersonal and public speaking.

Reception, Perception, Interpretation

If hearing isn't listening, what is listening? Listening includes three interwoven processes: (1) the physical reception of auditory stimuli, (2) the perception (symbolic classification) of the stimuli, and (3) the interpretation of the stimuli. The first has to do with the ears' ability to pick up sound-wave stimulation and carry it to the brain. The second process has to do with the brain's ability to select, organize, and symbolically categorize the stimuli brought to it through the hearing mechanisms. The third, the interpretive process, refers to the assignment of meaning* to the sounds, including the assessment of intent and suggestions for personal action. Listening is more than hearing, since it requires the categorization and interpretation of auditory stimuli as well as their reception (Harwood in Duker, 1966). Listening, then, is a complex skill made up of three basic stages. The last two, perception and interpretation, have the most importance for our analysis. Let's briefly look at them.

Perception is the selection, organization, and categorization of stimuli. When we listen, we do not attend to all of the sounds in our environment. Instead, we select certain sounds to which we pay attention. The sounds we select are partially determined

---

* Recall our earlier distinction between perception and the placing of symbol categorization into relational frameworks, i.e., the assignment of meaning.

by our expectations for the situation in which we find ourselves. The football player, interested in hearing the quarterback's signals, may not "hear" the noise of the crowd. Or, two people walking and talking on the streets of New York may be so wrapped up in their conversation, that they do not "hear" the noise of the city. But, people do more than simply select some auditory stimuli to attend to and reject others. We organize the stimulation selected into recognizable patterns. We don't hear a collection of isolated sounds, we hear words and sentences. A visitor to our country from the Far East remarked that Americans are difficult to understand. The reason he gave was that we "run our words together." He was saying that he was not attuned to picking out words from the flow of sounds that were coming from our mouths as we talked in everyday conversations. Say the following word to yourself: howyougonnakeepemdownonthefarm. Easy for us to comprehend; difficult for someone who is struggling to identify words.

As we organize, we categorize the stimuli into classes of auditory cues. When I hear a prolonged whistle as the sun is hanging just above the treetops, I know it is 6 o'clock. Why? Because I recognize the sound of the steam whistle of a local industry, which always blasts at 6 o'clock in the evening. If I hear a prolonged deep-throated hoot near 2 a.m., I know that the CNO freight is passing through town (and nearly on time). Why? Because the prolonged deep-throated hoot I categorize as a train call, hooting when the 1:45 freight rumbles through the city.

So far we have described the perception of auditory stimulus. Sounds are heard; we select some sounds to attend to out of all the sounds that come to us; these are categorized and organized into a recognizable pattern. Listening requires one more step: interpretation of the sound. That is, the relationship between me and what I hear is determined and some course of action is chosen concerning the sound. So, when I hear the sound in the late afternoon, I identify it as the work whistle (categorization), and know I ought to be heading home (interpretation). Or, I hear the sound at 2 a.m. (categorization), and I know the train is passing (interpretation) and I ought to go to bed if I'm going to be alive and alert for an 8 a.m. class (interpretation). How I interpret auditory stimuli will be affected by my emotional state, my motivation for attending to the stimuli, my knowledge level, and my past experiences. So, I can use my ears to monitor the sounds of my environment in order to keep me attuned to what's going on around me. I can receive the sound and categorize it, that is, label and classify it. However, such monitoring is a fairly passive information-processing.

Active Listening

To listen (to interpret), requires that I become an active participant in the auditory stimulation of the environment. In an interpersonal setting, listening requires my involvement with another as I attempt to determine what his utterances have to do with me, how he sees himself in a relationship with me, and what actions I should take in response to what he has said. People who believe Myth 3 forget the interpretation stage in the process. They see listening as the passive monitoring of the environment for information, while we see listening as categorization plus the active interpretation of the cues.

Active listening requires that one become involved with the speaker. The active listener is one who "listens to the words of others, but he also listens to the messages that are buried in the words encoated in all the cues that surround the words" (Egan, 1970, p. 248). The active listener attends to not only the auditory cues but also all behavioral cues emitted by the other—gesture, vocabulary, posture, facial expression, tone, rhythm, quality of voice, dress, and silences. At first glance such a statement about active listening may seem to push the concept of listening too far. But remember, listening goes beyond hearing, beyond perception and categorization, to interpretation. The more data we can collect, the more accurate and proper will be our interpretation of the words and what we should do about them. The interpretation of what I hear, determining what it means to me, what it means to us, and how I ought to respond, requires that I listen to all the cues the other person emits, in order to see the "idea and attitude from the other person's point-of-view, to sense how it feels to him, to achieve his frame of reference in regard to the thing he is talking about" (Rogers, 1961, p. 332). The more data I gather concerning the message and how the speaker feels about the message, the more likely I am to accurately interpret his message.

Listening is active involvement in the words and activities of another person. In a very real sense, listening as described here, is the sine qua non of interpersonal communication: without active listening, there could be no sharing of meanings.

REASONS PEOPLE ARE NOT GOOD LISTENERS

If listening is so important to us in our communication with others, why are we not good listeners? To answer that question, let's look at three characteristics of people which affect their listening: capacity to listen, willingness, and habits (Weaver, 1972). Each one of these characteristics gives us clues as to why people are not good listeners.

Capacity

The first characteristic, *capacity,* deals with the functioning of the individual's hearing mechanism, including the connection between the ear and the brain. If for some reason there is damage to the hearing mechanism, then our capacity to listen is lessened. This can occur through natural causes such as genetic defect or aging. Damage to the hearing mechanism (particularly the nerves) can also come from unnatural sources. Some of these defects are noise-induced and may result from prolonged exposure to snowmobile and motorcycle motors, firing guns, and even from the amplification of rock bands. Colds and throat and ear infections can also cause hearing loss. While this type of loss may be only temporary, it can still interfere with the capacity to hear, and therefore, the capacity to listen to another person.

There can be a loss in the capacity to listen because of "central deafness," the inability to process the auditory data gathered by the hearing mechanism. Stroke victims often have hearing problems. The difficulty has nothing to do with the hearing mechanism itself, but with the brain's ability to process the information sent to it on the auditory nerves. Senility in the aged can lead to a decrease in brain functioning: the ability to hear is not impaired, but the ability to process auditory information is.

Inadequacy of experience and language can affect the capacity to listen. Remember, listening requires interpretation. Interpretation requires language. If an individual lacks the language to categorize and interpret sounds, then he will be deficient in his capacity to listen. Because they develop a larger vocabulary to help categorize events, and because they have more experiences which permit them to symbolically interpret the auditory stimulation, children become better listeners as they grow (Weaver, 1972). Our capacity to hear affects our ability to listen.

Willingness

We are not good listeners because we are *unwilling to listen*. Several different examples are applicable here. One reason we are unwilling to listen to another is "our very natural tendency to judge, to evaluate, to approve or disapprove, the statement of another person" (Rogers, 1961, p. 330). That is, we tend to make judgments of goodness/badness, approval/disapproval of the words expressed by another person. We then react to our evaluation and not necessarily to what the other individual is saying to us.

===

INSIGHT 3.2   From *On Becoming a Person* by Carl R. Rogers*

I would like to propose, as an hypothesis for consideration, that the major barrier to mutual interpersonal communication is our very natural tendency to judge, to evaluate, to approve or disapprove, the statement of the other person, or the other group. Let me illustrate my meaning with some very simple examples. As you leave the meeting tonight, one of the statements you are likely to hear is, "I didn't like that man's talk." Now what do you respond? Almost invariably your reply will be either approval or disapproval of the attitude expressed. Either you respond, "I didn't either. I thought it was terrible," or else you tend to reply, "Oh, I thought it was really good." In other words, your primary reaction is to evaluate what has just been said to you, to evaluate it from *your* point-of-view, your own frame of reference.

Or take another example. Suppose I say with some feeling, "I think the Republicans are behaving in ways that show a lot of good sound sense these days," what is the response that arises in your mind as you listen? The overwhelming likelihood is that it will be evaluative. You will find yourself agreeing, or disagreeing, or making some judgment about me such as "He must be a conservative," or "He seems solid in his thinking." Or let us take an illustration from the international scene. Russia says vehemently, "The treaty with Japan is a war plot on the part of the United States." We rise as one person to say "That's a lie!"

This last illustration brings in another element connected with my hypothesis. Although the tendency to make evaluations is common in almost all interchanges of language, it is very much heightened in those situations where feelings and emotions are deeply involved. So the stronger our feelings the more likely it is that there will be no mutual element in the communication. There will be just two ideas, two feelings, two judgments, missing each other in psychological space. I'm sure you recognize this from your own experience. When you have not emotionally involved yourself, and have listened to a heated discussion, you often go away thinking, "Well, they actually weren't talking about the same thing." And they were not. Each was making a judgment, an evaluation, from his own frame of reference. There was really nothing which could be called communication in any genuine sense. This tendency to react to any emotionally meaningful statement by forming an evaluation of it from our point-of-view, is, I repeat, the major barrier to interpersonal communication.

* Carl R. Rogers, *On Becoming a Person* (Boston: Houghton Mifflin, 1961), pp. 330–331.

The following exchange was recently overheard while attending a performance of *A Midsummer Night's Dream* at a Shakespearean drama festival:

He: "How did you like the production? (in a halting manner with a quiet voice)

She: "Well, I don't know. The maidservant was delightful, but the rest . . . didn't seem real."

He: "You should have read the play and a synopsis first. I don't think you understood the whole thing." (He is not responding to her, but to his evaluation of her statement. He sees her as not liking the production because she didn't understand, because she isn't too well-read, because she doesn't like to read, because she was brought up by ill-bred parents, because they . . .)

You can imagine the discussion that ensued. By the time they were one-half block from the theater, they were arguing about their in-law relationships and not about their reactions to the play.

Evaluating is a natural human reaction. We want to determine whether something is desirable or not. The problem comes when we don't listen to one another, when we don't understand the other's point-of-view, or frame of reference, before making an evaluation.

Another reason we are unwilling to listen is that we don't want to know what we might hear if we were to listen. Ever try to recall what a police officer said to you after pulling you over on the shoulder of a highway? Oh, you might have an impression of what he said. But, you really don't want to hear that you have broken the law, that your action has endangered the lives of others, that this ticket is for your benefit, that the justice of the peace is open all night, that you aren't very careful, that . . . So, if I expect to hear noxious material, then I have a tendency not to listen. There are plenty of politicians throughout this country, on the right and on the left, who were voted out of office, or were never voted in, because people never listened to their positions.

People cannot listen to others when they are wrapped up in themselves. We become so interested in what we are going to say, that we just do no pay any attention to what the other person is saying or doing.

> The reason that no one listens, usually is that our egos get in the way, in the sense that we're mentally formulating what *we're* going to say when the other person gets through speaking. Instead of digesting the other person's information, we are most often busy thinking only of how we can *impress* him with our next statement (Addeo and Burger, 1973, p. xiii).

The situation described is called EgoSpeak. The point made is well taken: nobody listens to you because you don't listen to anybody else. (See Insight 3.3.) We're so wrapped up in ourselves, *our* thoughts, *our* problems, *our* contributions, that we don't listen.

INSIGHT 3.3   From *EgoSpeak* by Edmond G. Addeo and
Robert E. Burger*

Think about how often you *speak* from the time you awaken to the time you go to sleep. The answer psychologists give is approximately *seven hundred* discrete utterings, that is, those which aren't parts of a "conversation" but actually different occasions to say something. Investigators say some people utter 12,000 sentences every day, which averages out to almost 100,000 words!

Put differently, an average American can speak the equivalent of two novels per day, although he *reads* less than three books per year.

We seem to be so busy "speaking" to each other that we're not really "saying" very much. Conversation, or the art of such, is being "lost" only because no one is *listening*. And no one is listening to *you* because *you* haven't listened to the other guy.

Often we're wrapped up in ourselves because of physical discomfort. For instance, I've never liked teaching an 11 a.m. class. People are so hungry and restless by 11:45 that the last few minutes of class are lost to any useful activity. Sometimes we're so emotionally involved in ourselves that there is no energy left to listen to someone else. Isn't it hard to attend to a history lecture at 9 a.m., when you're to have a math midterm at 10 a.m.? Sometimes the discomfort comes from the experience itself. Have you ever found it hard to sustain a conversation with others while waiting in a dentist's office? Some people are so frightened by the dentist that they can't hear you. Or, take the difficulty of listening to a person with an unpleasant voice: e.g., a woman with a particularly shrill voice, or a man who speaks in a monotone. The sounds themselves are disconcerting, the voice unpleasant, and listening becomes difficult. Hearing takes place, but listening is hampered. Our unwillingness prevents us from listening to people.*

Habits

Finally, our *listening habits* prevent us from listening. Our culture is word-oriented. We often become so intent upon hearing the content of words, we miss the other cues which may tell us the emotional state of the individual, how he thinks about us and our relationship. This isn't surprising because we are an idea culture and words carry ideas. Our TV, films and literature are filled with examples of this and so is our everyday life. Have you ever been so busy taking notes in class that you missed the point of the lecture? Although you may have recorded every word, much of the speaker's meaning was probably transmitted in his actions and voice quality.

In your schooling, have you ever had a course in listening? A number of studies have been done on how much time an individual spends on the four major communication activities each day. The studies show that we spend the following percentages of our time on each of the following communication activities: reading, 16%; writing, 9%; talking, 30%; listening, 45% (Weaver, 1972, p. 13). Isn't it ironic that our schooling places so much emphasis on writing, which takes the least amount of our communication time, and spends virtually no time teaching listening, the skill in which we spend approximately one-half of our waking hours?**

√Another habit which prevents people from listening is that we can survive without having to listen. Parents and teachers

---

*For an interesting account of human unwillingness to listen read: Addeo and Burger, *EgoSpeak,* 1973.

**Later in this chapter, we'll suggest some techniques for improving listening. For a more thorough discussion, see Egan, *Encounter,* pp. 248-282; Weaver, *Human Listening,* chapters 4 and 5, pp. 82-123; Irvin, "Activities Designed to Improve Listening Skill," *Journal of Communication,* IV (1954), p. 14.

can do a lot to teach a child not to listen. Telling your daughter to pick up her room, and then, when she doesn't, doing it yourself, teaches her not to pay attention to you. Telling your son, who's dressed in his Sunday school best, to go inside and change clothes before he plays, and then ignoring him when he doesn't do it, teaches him not to listen to you. Recently, an elementary teacher confessed that she made a number of corrections for the students in their math notebooks before they were taken home. The reason? She was trying to prevent the children from being punished at home for doing inaccurate work. "Sometimes I don't give directions well," she said. Maybe the problem isn't her directions at all, but the fact that the student is never asked to suffer the consequences of not paying attention to those instructions.

Social reinforcement encourages us to form the habit of speaking and not listening. Don't we often make the "active conversationalist" the center of our attention? In schools, isn't it usually the student who holds up his hand that receives the approval of the teacher? Granted, it's hard to tell what is going on in the mind of the quiet student. But, isn't it possible that the quiet one is listening? For example, I am often jolted by how much my son remembers of Disneyland, which he visited when he was three years old: though while we were at the fabulous park, he seemed quiet, almost aloof, and my wife and I were concerned that he wasn't enjoying himself. Several times we tried to get him to talk about what he was experiencing, but he flipped us off with one or two words. A week later, on the lap of his aunt who asked him what he saw at Disneyland, he reported in great detail the sights and sounds of the Magic Kingdom. More than three years later, he still talks about his perceptions of Tomorrowland and Adventureland. What we interpreted as a state of being overwhelmed or even disinterested was really a state of total absorption in what was going on around him.

Every day, the American public is bombarded with auditory stimuli. Radio tells us to buy; television asks us to be involved; spouses ask for affection; children cry for attention; neighbors gossip; salespeople pitch; ministers, teachers, and politicians all clamor. To get some peace of mind, to get some time for reflection, to protect ourselves from overstimulation and information overload, we train ourselves to "tune out." A lot of people are sending messages to us, but "they ain't nobody home." The husband hiding behind his evening newspaper while the wife chatters away about the events of the day is a classic cartoon motif. Like that husband, we all periodically shut our eyes, ears, and other senses to what is going on around us in order to wrap ourselves in quiet. Sometimes, we tune out by tuning in—the radio or television. Adults laugh about the lack of conversation around TV sets these days and the high levels of amplification that teenagers use to play their records. While all of this noise can't be attributed to the habit of tuning out, certainly some of it is just that. The point is, we develop the habit of tuning out in order to avoid listening. Unfortunately, this habit can carry over into situations where we may want to listen, but the skills, sensitivity, and awareness have been dulled by inactivity. Our capacity to hear, our willingness to listen, and our listening habits provide three general areas which exemplify why we are poor listeners.

LISTENING DEMANDS RESPONSE

We've taken our definition of listening beyond the simple reception of sound, to include the perception and interpretation of cues emitted by another. But, how do we know when we are listening or when others are listening to us? The ultimate proof of listening is the translation of what has been heard into effective interaction (Egan, 1972, p. 259). Eric Berne, the father of Transactional Analysis, says, "Proper listening is manifested by giving the right response" (Berne, 1965, p. 71). Using the words of Kelly, who more closely approximates our definition of communication-states, ". . . listening by its very nature has to be empathetic; a person understands what he has heard only to the extent that he can share in the meaning, spirit, or feeling of what the communicator has said" (Kelly, 1970, p. 253).

In other words, people know if they've been listened to by the response they get. If this is true, then listening and its

59

manifest response become the keys to establishing a state of communication: listening and its consequent actions become the method for recognizing whether or not mutual understanding has occurred. Or, to say it in a different manner, listening is a necessary condition for understanding and being understood: it is a necessary ingredient for developing a communication-state.

INSIGHT 3.4   From *Yak, Yak, Yak . . . How EgoSpeak Has Ruined Our Ability to Listen* by E. G. Addeo and R. E. Burger*

Another way of putting it, the art of communication is actually an art of love, the art of saying something you mean to someone, something which you dearly and sincerely want him to know. You want him to know it because it is something you want to share. When this art is practised, listening is made tolerable for others. Then conversation becomes an interaction which leaves both participants with a feeling of satisfaction and fulfillment. You might even hear that rare compliment—"I enjoyed talking to you."

* From *EgoSpeak: Why No One Listens to You.* Copyright © 1973 by Edmond G. Addeo and Robert E. Burger. Reprinted with permission of the publisher, Chilton Book Company, Radnor, Pa. 19089. As reprinted in the Detroit Free Press, 1974.

The manifestation of listening is the response one makes to another. That response we call feedback.

FEEDBACK AND ITS FUNCTIONS

Feedback is the listener's response, perceived and interpreted by the speaker as relevant to the message and social setting. The response can be verbal and nonverbal. What is important is whether or not the source of the original message (the speaker) interprets, and finds the response relevant to his message and to the social setting.

There is a problem with discussing feedback, because we have to look at one participant at a time, even though we know that each participant is both source and receiver simultaneously. Each is responding to the other as the other is responding and seeing himself responded to. Keep in mind that what we are discussing is happening simultaneously.

The Source

From the point of view of the source, feedback serves a corrective function. The responses he sees and interprets tell him "how he is doing," on both the content and relational levels of his message. If the listener is sitting comfortably, leans forward, smiles and nods his head in approval, then the source may think that "everything is fine, he understands, he agrees, and finds the relationship acceptable." In this case, we would not expect to see changes occur in the message-sending behavior or in the relationship.

If the listener fidgets, leans back with his arms folded, frowns occasionally, shakes his head, then stands up and walks around, the source may think that he "isn't getting through." Either the listener doesn't understand, doesn't agree, or doesn't believe that the source has the right, within their relationship, to talk about these things. The reactions of the listener are interpreted by the source as negative. When feedback is interpreted as negative, some changes usually occur in either the method of presentation, the topics discussed, or the relational definition. So, feedback provides the source with information about the acceptability of his ideas, his topic, his right to discuss the topic, and the amount of control he has over the situation. Feedback provides an answer to the implicit question, "How am I doing?"

The Receiver

From the point of view of the receiver, feedback serves a control function. The responses he transmits influence the subsequent behaviors of the speaker. Recall the listener descriptions above. In both cases, the listener influenced the behavior of the source (who changed or did not change his behavior) and exerted control over their relationship. The act of feeding back is the way the receiver assumes his active, responsible role in the communication process and in the establishment of a communication-state. As an active participant, the receiver influences both the messages transmitted and the rules governing the relationship. Listening (hearing and response) is the key to a communication-state.

Without the response, neither interactant can know if he is understood, if he understands the other, if the relationship is acceptable to both, and if each participant is accepted by the other. To refuse to give active responses (which in itself is a kind of feedback) is to reduce the influence one has as a receiver, over the other, the relationship and the situation. Refusal eliminates the opportunity to mutually understand one another, and effectively removes the chance for a communication-state between participants. If the receiver is then unhappy with the consequences, it is his own fault he didn't assume his responsibility for the communication event and relationship.

The listener has an infinite number of possible responses to feedback to the speaker—think of them as falling along an acceptance-rejection continuum. The rejection responses will not be discussed here, as they might only help to perpetuate the communication myths.*

SUPPORTIVE RESPONSES

In explaining supportive responses, two aspects of feedback need to be identified: (1) the intention of the listener in responding, and (2) the method of stating the response (Johnson, 1972). The *intention* of the feedback refers to the reasons for sending the message, and the portion of the speaker's message to which the response is directed. The *method of stating response* refers to the messages chosen (both verbal and nonverbal), the means of presenting the messages, and their arrangement. Perhaps an example of nonsupportive response may help to clarify the two aspects of supportive response.

---

*For a discussion of negative responses read: Berne, *Games People Play;* Goffman, *The Presentation of Self in Everyday Life;* Bach and Wyden, *The Intimate Enemy.*

In many homes, the wife takes charge of the financial affairs including budgeting, bill-paying, record-keeping, and weekly allocations of spending money. Sometimes the husband has an idea about how the money ought to be spent or budgeted, and he says:

Honey, have you ever thought of paying for some of the household purchases by cash instead of using credit cards? These bills get so large with presents and major purchases. We could keep them under control and cut our finance charges, too, if we did.

The content of the message expresses a mild criticism for charging most household items, some of which do not need to be charged. The relationship dimension assumes the wife has had, and will continue to have, control of the financial affairs. However, in making his suggestion, the husband asserts that he, too, has the right to influence financial decisions and procedures. The wife replies:

I'm the one who pays the bills. I know how much money we have and what we have to live on each month. Sometimes I *have* to charge household stuff or we wouldn't have any cash. That means no golf, no Scotch, no movies—all things *you* like. Let me worry about it!

The content of the wife's message is an explanation for the charging practices, given as an answer to the criticism. She makes the assumption that the husband doesn't know all the circumstances and so speaks uninformed. The relationship dimension of the message speaks to another matter. The emphasis on "I," the references to her responsibility, her worry, and her knowledge indicate she does not consider him her equal when it comes to money matters. She is saying, "This is my area of expertise. You keep out!"

He reacts, "For Chrissake! I just made a suggestion. You don't have to have a hemorrhage!" The content of his response withdraws the original suggestion. The relationship dimension displayed in the voice volume, tone, and quicker rhythm indicates irritation. The husband asserted himself as an equal in the financial affairs of the family, and his effort was rebuked:

his competence and right to speak on this matter was rejected.

This example illustrates the two dimensions of messages that are responded to constantly. It also shows that the interpretation of these responses at these two levels may be different, i.e., willingness to withdraw the suggestion on charge cards, but irritation at the rejection of equality of financial control in the relationship.

The example also demonstrates another point—supportive responses rest upon the assumptions of mutual respect and trust. (Trust will be discussed more in Chapter 5.) Each person must accept the other as a unique individual who has worth and who has the right within their relationship to speak about the topic under consideration. If one cannot be accepted and respected as a unique person with worth, there isn't any support in the relationship. Furthermore, relational rules, which permit people to discuss their feelings toward each other, need to be created in a relationship.

Let's not get confused about respect. People can respect each other as unique and worthwhile human beings and still disagree. We can respect each other without liking one another, without being socially close, or madly in love. The point is that supportive response rests upon the assumption of mutual respect.

Styles of Supportive Response

How can we improve as listener/responders to better ensure that a supportive interpersonal climate will be created? Borrowing from Johnson (1972), we suggest three response styles which help to create supportive climates between people. The three styles are called *supportive, probing* and *understanding*.

In using the supportive style, the listener intends to "reassure, to pacify, to reduce the sender's intensity of feeling" (Johnson, 1972, p. 125). The response supports because the listener is attempting to display empathy toward the speaker and to encourage the speaker to reduce the intensity of his emotion. After the emotional intensity is reduced, then, together, they can take constructive action to correct the problem, if a problem exists. Or, they can simply explore mutual feelings, their emotional roots, and the behavioral consequences in order for understanding to occur.

In using the probing style, the listener questions the speaker with the intent of gathering additional information (Johnson, 1972). While obtaining additional information, the probing response also encourages more discussion, since a question usually requests an answer. Implicit in probing is the withholding of evaluation. Evaluation breeds defensiveness, while probing demonstrates interest, concern, and support.

When using the understanding style, the listener intends to demonstrate that he understands what the speaker is saying (Johnson, 1972). In practice, the understanding style can be a paraphrase of the implicit and explicit remarks of the speaker, responding to either the content or the relationship dimension of the message. Let's explore an example to demonstrate the three styles.

"I get so tired of the same thing on every date. Why does everybody think we have to hit the sack? I don't want to, haven't, and am not going to. Can't anybody just go out and have fun anymore?"

Supportive response: "Lots of people feel the same way. I do. Just get with people who feel like you do. I could fix you up . . ."

Probing response: "What happened tonight that makes you feel this way?"

Understanding response: "You're angry that too many people consider a good time as having sex. You're annoyed that people don't seem to want to just have fun."

Notice that all three styles are essentially *descriptive* of the behavior and feelings of the other. *No judgment* of the other is made, at least, not at the time of the response. The individual is accepted and respected as unique.

We have said many times that the act of response implies some equality and acceptance of the other, and mutual respect. In other words, developing and using these three response styles in everyday conversation can help us become more supportive of others. Support usually encourages support from the other. With

65

mutual support the chance for more accurate self-conceptions and more satisfying interpersonal relations increases.

WAYS TO OVERCOME THE MYTH

1. Take the time and expend the energy to listen to others rather than merely hearing them. The following suggestions may help:

a. When someone talks to you look them in the face. Forcing yourself to attend to the face (where the words emerge from) may help you to attend to what they say. If you let your eyes move around the environment you often become distracted.

b. The next time someone talks to you, force yourself to remove distractions. If you're at your desk, move away from it so you won't be tempted to "keep working" (if only mentally). If you're doing something you can't stop (at a crucial point in preparing dinner) tell the other person you can't listen then; that you want to listen, and that when you're finished the two of you will sit down to talk. This is particularly important in dealing with children. They need to know you have your life to lead but that it is one which includes them. They will respect your wishes if you'll respect theirs. Honesty is important in human relationships. Better to have the other person suffer a momentary hurt in exchange for your full interest later than to be misled into believing you care while you really tune-out.

c. When listening to someone try to: listen for the major ideas; listen for the emotional state of the speaker; and assess the ideas presented in light of the emotions. For example, when your roommate asks you to "go for a coke," is the intent to quench thirst or eliminate loneliness?

2. Describe behaviors, events and attitudes in your own language. Evaluation is important and natural to man, but evaluation ought to be delayed until each participant understands, and knows that the other understands what has been

said. Alternatives ought to be explored. Then, evaluation can take place and each will know what is being evaluated and why. Haim Ginott called this sticking to the behaviors, the "single most important rule" for speaking to children, particularly when giving them praise (Ginott, 1965, p. 39).

a. The next time someone does something you like, tell them precisely what they did that you liked, and why. For example, a friend takes a phone call and leaves a note with all the information needed for you to return the call. Tell the person, "Thank you for taking the message. I liked the completeness of the information. It made it easy for me to take care of my business. I like your doing nice things for me." In this message you (a) specify the behavior you saw and liked, (b) indicate you liked it, and (c) identify what you liked about the behavior. Your friend knows what was done that you appreciated, and why.

b. Withhold your evaluation of another person's position until you are sure you understand it. This is most difficult: we want to evaluate and respond. But hold it! The best practice is to paraphrase the remarks of the other before making your point—paraphrasing is the Understanding response described earlier. Say, "I hear you saying . . ." or "I think you're trying to say . . ." or "Check my understanding, but I think you're telling me . . ." You'll find you listen more attentively if you make yourself respond in this manner, and you'll reduce the number of arguments caused by misunderstanding—particularly those senseless arguments often caused by using common words which have several meanings.

3. Use specific language to which the speaker can supply meaning. Concrete, specific language is considered one of the important core dimensions of responding (Gazda, 1973). The more specific the language of the response, the more vivid will be the mental images of the speaker. These can be checked against your own images through listening and feedback.

To understand the process more fully try the following exercise. Create a speech which emphasizes specific, vivid language. Your objective is to stimulate mental images in your audience. The topic of the speech should be something concrete; i.e., the description of some process like the making of plastic, the refining of oil to gasoline, or the stalking of steelhead fishing holes. Divide the topic into time units to make sure that you follow the process through its chronological development. Without the use of visual aids, describe the entire process step-by-step. You may want to create a manuscript for this speech. If you do, attempt to eliminate all "to be" verbs, use colorful modifiers, and comparisons and contrasts instead. Check to see how clear the mental images are by asking the audience to write a description of what they saw while you spoke, or by asking them to draw some portion of the process. Perhaps different parts of the audience might draw different aspects of the process. Art isn't important—the audience's conceptualization is.

4. Accurately and precisely state to the speaker what you are thinking and feeling about the content and relationship. What you intend to convey in your response, and to what you are responding, should be as obvious to the speaker as you can make them. Accuracy requires that you think about what you will say, and listen to yourself to see if you are saying what you want to. Observe your body and voice to see that your physical behavior complements your language.

5. Develop listening skills for public speaking. Here are two key comments about listening to a public speaker: (a) avoid evaluation before the speaker has had a chance to completely develop his theme for you and (b) use the time differential (the difference between the speaking rate and the brain rate) to increase your knowledge of the points of the speaker. The first is merely withholding judgment—a suggestion we've made for interpersonal settings as well—until the speaker is finished and you can verbalize his major themes and reasons. To that end, using your time well will assist you in being able to verbalize the speaker's points. For example, listen for the speaker's main theme and put it into your own words; identify his reasons for the theme, also in your own words; identify the principle bits of evidence the speaker uses to prove his point. Ask yourself: is the evidence relevant to the reason given? Is the evidence consistent with other information I have? from where does his

evidence come? the speaker's experience? some authority? As you listen, reconstruct the speech in your own mind with the theme, reasons and important bits of evidence. Once you're sure you know what the speaker is talking about, evaluate what he is saying in light of what you know and believe.

Do the above with your class while listening to a series of speeches (at a debate, or PTA, or sales meeting, etc.). Check your mental outline of the speech with those of your friends. You'll be interested to see the different interpretations, and you should also see a difference between the friends who listened to and those who only heard the speech.

There are many other suggestions that could be offered, but if we practice these few more often, we will all become better at developing communication-states.* The best single step to take in improving as a listener is to reject the myth which says that hearing is listening.

Remember, listening requires a capacity first, then a willingness, and then the cultivation of habits which improve listening. If you have the capacity, energy is needed to be willing to listen. The habits which decrease our willingness to listen can be broken by practicing the response styles suggested and improving the phrasing of verbal responses.

SUMMARY

Our society holds with the myth that to hear someone is to listen to him. This belief presupposes that if people would just use their ears, they would hear and understand. Such a belief assumes that communication is a one-way transmission of messages, that hearing the message is synonymous with understanding it. The myth in this chapter complements the one described in chapter 1. The difference is that chapter 1 took the sender's point of view, while this chapter takes the receiver's point of view.

---

*See Gazda (1973), Keltner (1970), and Johnson (1972) for detailed directions for improving the responding necessary for listening.

In attempting to dispel the myth, we have suggested that listening includes the reception of sound, the classification of the sound into symbolic categories, and the interpretation of the sounds based on those categories. Further, how we listen to one another is affected by our capacity to hear, our willingness to listen, and our listening habits. But, listening in interpersonal encounters goes beyond the mere reception of sound: communication, the mutual sharing of meaning, can occur only if the listener understands the speaker and vice-versa. Understanding and being understood, requires that each respond to the other, that each provide feedback for the other. This is the only way interactants can know they have shared meanings.

We have suggested that people can improve their ability to understand by withholding their tendency to judge others (evaluate them); encouraging the other by probing his messages; supporting the other's emotions; and checking our interpretations of what the other is saying. The receiver can only assume his responsibility for building a communication-state by responding after he has listened.

Why should we work so hard to reach a communication-state? Forget for the moment the delight of deeper relationships. We need to expend the energies to improve our abilities to make contact with others, because who we are grows from how we relate to others. Selfishly, then, we have reason to improve our message behaviors—our self-concept is at stake.

4

NONVERBAL
AND BEHAVIOR
COMMUNICATION

MYTH

*"Every Little Movement
Has a Meaning All its Own!"**

In a recent class, we discussed nonverbal behavior and the way in which actions affect human connection. The following day, several students brought in magazine articles, all of which implied that we can "read" the body language of others. One girl mentioned that a guy in the front row was "telling" the people on his right that he was "excluding them" from the conversation. She "knew" this because he was sitting with his right leg crossed over his left with the toes of the right leg pointing left and turned away from his right side. The guy laughed and said:

> "Hell, I've got knee injuries from football. I've had so many knee operations . . . I cross my right over my left because I *can't* cross my legs any other way. It hurts even now to have them crossed at all, so I don't do it much. Believe me, babe, if you were sitting on my right and thought you were being excluded because of the way I crossed my legs, then . . . well, . . . *you'd* have a problem!"

---

*From an article, "Every Little Movement Has a Meaning All Its Own . . ." by Flora Davis, *Woman's Day*, Sept. 1972, pp. 64, 116–118.

Recent popular literature suggests to the reader that every movement has a meaning. Such literature claims that we can "read" others, if we just watch them, that we can "influence" them if we carefully control our body actions. But, in order to be able to read and influence, we would have to assume that motions have the same meanings across persons and social situations, and that all observers would arrive at the same interpretation of the behavior. Of course, even if some motions are unintentional, we would have to view them as revealing the "true" person. So, we attend to those we know are "true" and ignore those movements that we know the other person knows we might be attending to, and therefore, is controlling. The point is that there exists a myth in our culture that every action has a meaning. Research doesn't support such an all-encompassing conclusion. We call it a "myth" because the process of interpreting movements is complex.

PROBLEMS OF INTERPRETATION

One problem with interpreting nonverbal behaviors is the nature of the perception process. While an infinite number of behavioral and environmental cues may be available to the senses, the brain will monitor and interpret only those it attends to and those which it has language to categorize. It's been estimated that the eye can handle about five million bits of information per second, but the brain can process only approximately 500 bits per second. So, "selection is inevitable" (Haney, 1967, p. 53). Hundreds of thousands of cues can be given off by a person and the environment—muscle tension, eye blinks, eye contact, leg position, hand movements, posture, dress, body type, complexion, distance, room arrangement, temperature—but the individual may perceive only one general behavioral area. The perceptual process prevents us from observing and interpreting all of the nonverbal behavior around us.

What is interpreted and how, develops from what the observer attends to, and not necessarily from the nonverbal cue. Therefore, you might intentionally want me to notice the decreased distance between us, which you've arranged. But,

I notice your clothes and hair. Because we are focusing on two different things, a misunderstanding can be created—I react to the clothes, while you may assume I'm responding to the distance.* What is perceived and interpreted, then, will vary with the observer. So, to assert that your rhythmic leg movement is going to help you get your man, is, at best, shaky. He might not see the leg movement at all, because of the strand of spaghetti caught between your two front teeth, which spoils your smile.

Suppose that observers all attend to the same cues and all neglect the same behaviors. We would still find a problem with interpreting the nonverbal, and hence, have trouble in developing, between us, similar meanings for the behaviors. Nonverbal behavior is ambiguous. Why? For many of the same reasons we gave when discussing the problem of meaning in verbal language. The meaning we assign to a nonverbal cue is situation-bound; meanings for nonverbal cues are learned; meanings we assign to nonverbal cues will change over time as our social experiences change us; no two people have the same meaning for the same nonverbal cue.

Finally, the interpretation of nonverbal behavior is ambiguous because the cues are not readily translated into language (Watzlawick et al., 1967). Think of the number of different kinds of smiles you've seen. Yet, how many different words do you have to describe the number of facial configurations we generally label as "smile"? We use words, which are discrete categories, to describe behavior, which is continuous. For example, imagine that a couple gets into heavy making-out one evening. The skin of the girl becomes moist, the hands slightly shaking, the lips moist and moderately trembling, the feet and ankles constantly moving, the legs become rigid as if the knees won't bend, the breathing shallows and increases in rate, her back develops tension which arches the back and pushes the breasts upward into her partner. What do these behaviors mean? She is willing to engage in sexual intercourse? She is frightened? In pain? We could assign any of these three meanings to the behaviors described and be correct, depending upon the relationship, the girl, the setting, etc. But, notice the number of

---

*For an extended examination of perception, see M. D. Vernon, *Psychology of Perception,* 1962.

words it took to describe the girl's nonverbal behaviors and we haven't even begun to describe all of the subtle physical changes taking place.

For some nonverbal behaviors, our culture has developed ritualized patterns which have particular, agreed upon meaning. This reduces the ambiguity of interpretation, since we (within a group or a culture) agree on what the behavior "means." For example, we agree that tilting the head up-and-down vigorously means "yes"; or, flopping the hand at the wrist, palm outward, means "goodby" (in some cultures, this movement means "hello"). Such rituals reduce ambiguity for some nonverbal actions or patterns. But, only a small number of possible nonverbal cues have become ritualized. In addition, ritualized behaviors may have been agreed upon by only a limited few, so that their meanings do not cross cultures or subcultures.

Nonverbal cues are difficult to interpret because: they do not readily translate into symbolic language; no two people have the same meaning; meanings change over time; they are learned; they are bound by the social context; there are so many cues that the brain is unable to monitor, categorize, and interpret all those available. Even though ambiguity exists in the interpretation of nonverbal cues they work with the verbal codes in order to create a total message. Working with the verbal code helps to reduce the ambiguity of each code and make the total message more easily interpretable by the observer.

NONVERBAL WORKS WITH THE VERBAL CODE

Researchers have catalogued ways in which the nonverbal and verbal messages work together to create a total message impression (Ekman and Friesen, in Tompkins and Izard, 1965). They are:

Repeating

The nonverbal behaviors repeat the substance of the verbal message. The body can repeat an emotion: a son or daughter weeps while talking about the grief felt when their parent died;

a fisherman talks about a three-foot steelhead, while demonstrating the length with his hands (the fish got away, of course); an American tourist describes the trajectory of the dives of the natives from the cliffs in Acapulco. In all these cases, the verbal content receives support through the repetition of the message by the nonverbal behaviors.

Substituting

The nonverbal behavior actually replaces the verbal portion of the message: forming a V with the fingers, indicating "peace" or "victory" (depending upon your generation). Nonverbal behaviors which substitute usually have a symbolic base, unlike behaviors that repeat, which need not have a symbolic base.

Accenting

The nonverbal behavior underscores parts of the verbal message much the way underlining or italicizing underscores the written word: the squeeze of the hand with "I love you"; the fist on the desk while shouting "damn!"; leaning toward another, saying "tell me, I'm interested." All these instances are ones in which the nonverbal accents the verbal message. The nonverbal behavior of the sender qualifies the verbal message: a blush, a laugh, shuffling feet, downcast eyes, all can tell the receiver how the sender is feeling about the message he is sending. In teasing, we use the nonverbal behavior to clue the receiver that the words are jesting jibes and not intended to hurt—the wink, the elbow jab to the ribs.

Regulating

The nonverbal behaviors of each of the participants maintain, interrupt, or change the transactional pattern. Eye contact, head nods, shifts of position, cigarette drags or puffs, can all serve to cue the other individual that it's their turn to speak. A gasp for air, a forward lean, a variety of hand movements, can all serve to clue the other person that you wish to have the floor. Looking or turning away, leaning back, lighting a cigarette, sipping your drink, can all be clues to stop the flow of messages, temporarily at least.

In public speaking chairs are positioned to focus audience attention on the speaker. Your attention is focused in one direction because your body faces that direction. You see backs of heads rather than faces. It is physically difficult and publicly obvious to speak with those behind you, and rudely inconvenient to speak with those sitting by your side more than one or two seats away. Therefore, the communication flow between audience members has been regulated.

Contradicting

The nonverbal behaviors are simultaneously inconsistent with the verbal message. A common example is a face with wrinkled brow, tearful eye, drooping mouth, and bitten lip, while the person mutters "Nothing" to the question, "Is anything wrong?" We don't believe the verbal in this case because of the contradiction between the face and the language.

In interpersonal communication settings, inconsistency creates confusion in the mind of the observer. What is the speaker trying to tell him? What should he believe? Mehrabian, a psychologist, suggests that we resolve the inconsistency between codes by believing the nonverbal portion of the total message (Mehrabian, 1971).

In our culture, expression of feelings is discouraged except with intimates. However, all of us experience feelings which require expression. Dual pressures mount within us: feelings demanding expression and social norms discouraging their expression. Being denied the verbal expression of feelings by social norms, the body expresses them more subtly in its movements and postures. So, nonverbal behaviors may contradict one another as the body displays two emotions at once. The observer may be thoroughly confused by the apparent discordance (Beier, 1974). Generally though, others weigh our actions more than our words as they try to understand what we feel (Mehrabian, 1971).

But there exists confusion and discomfort in a receiver of contradictory messages, even if the tendency is to believe the nonverbal behavior. However we interpret the total message (verbal and nonverbal), legitimate doubt (over and above the normal doubt that should exist) will linger when one level of the message contradicts the other. Thus, a dilemma exists for the receiver.

A special case of contradictory messages (the double-bind) has been suggested as a basis for schizophrenics. The following conditions are necessary for the double-bind theory to be applicable: (1) two or more persons in an important relationship; (2) a message structured so the parts are mutually exclusive—the parts contradict each other; (3) the recipient cannot withdraw from the relationship to eliminate the contradictory nature of the message. The recipient must act upon the message, yet to act appropriately to one portion of the message automatically means an incorrect action to the other part. The recipient is in a "bind." Doubly so, since either reaction is inappropriate.

An acute schizophrenic was recovering, when he was visited by his mother in the hospital. Glad to see her, he put his arm around her shoulders. She stiffened. He withdrew his arm. "Don't you love me anymore?" she asked. He blushed. Mother said, "Dear, you must not be so easily embarrassed and afraid of your feelings" (Bateson, in Jackson, 1968, p. 44). The relationship of mother to son is an important one. Her stiffening at his touch, and then asking for an expression of love, and then reprimanding him for both of his emotions (love and embarrassment), makes this an example of the double-bind situation. The bind may be thus: "If I am to keep my tie to mother, I must not show her I love her; but if I do not show her I love her, then I will lose her" (ibid., p. 45).

Notice that in the case of the double-bind, there is no way out. In contradictory or inconsistent messages, the recipient can choose correctly or incorrectly between the conflicting messages; but in a double-bind, there is no choice; no action is appropriate. For example:

He: "If you love me, show me. Let's 'make love.' "

She: Knows from his previous remarks, that he will not marry a girl who is not a virgin. Yet, does love him and wants to show him.

She is doubly bound; the relationship is important, but she has received two contradictory messages and either choice is inappropriate.

Why is the double-bind important to us? There are three reasons for including it in a basic interpersonal communications book. We are talking about creating important relationships between people. Our culture discourages the open expression of feelings.* Our culture encourages us to intentionally create contradictory messages. The habit can easily create situations in which we send messages that double-bind.

Earlier, we recommended that a speaker help reduce error and ambiguity in messages by attempting to ensure that the verbal and nonverbal message components be consistent. The reasoning behind this recommendation may be more clear now: at best, binding in a relationship breeds confusion and distrust; at the worst, a double-binding pattern of interaction encourages interpersonal pathologies.

KINDS OF NONVERBAL CUES IMPORTANT TO HUMAN RELATIONS

We've stressed the point that interpretation of nonverbal cues is ambiguous. However, controlled observation and research *have* isolated and identified some nonverbal behaviors which are consistently interpreted by observers in the same way. Remember that caution must be exercised in generalizing from the research because of the difficulties already listed. We present here only that work (experimental or observed) which is directly related to interpersonal communication. The nonverbal areas are: environment, space, physical appearance and dress, body movements, face, eyes, and touch.

Environment

That the environment exerts a tremendous influence on settings for human interaction seems obvious, yet it is often

---

*The open expression of feelings is a necessary condition for the creation of important relationships.

forgotten. In the northern states, several months of the year are cold and wet. People see one another while working or running errands. The casual encounter over the back fence or strolling at dusk is inhibited by the weather. In the warmer states, the casual encounter can occur even during the winter months, because people can be outdoors comfortably. This does not mean that people in southern states are more friendly or have more or deeper relationships. But, it does mean that the climate affects the frequency of interpersonal encounters.

Weather may indirectly affect message content by influencing how people feel physically. Correlations have been reported between high barometric pressure and the number of people who sought hospital help for depression. "Psychiatric admissions tended to increase on days with little sunshine, low temperatures and heavy pollution" (Detroit *Free Press,* May 10, 1974, p. 1A).

The physical arrangement of the environment affects human contact, and hence, the types and numbers of relationships which can be established and maintained. For example, people who live in houses in the middle of the block seem to have more contact than those whose homes are located elsewhere (Knapp, 1972). Interesting research on public housing in Chicago found that prejudice against the blacks was the least when white residents had the most or the least contact with blacks. Prejudice was most apparent when there was only a medium amount of contact (Grimshaw, 1969). The environment, influencing the amount of contact available between the races, seems to influence the relationships.

Often overlooked as a factor, the environment, including climate and neighborhood arrangement, can influence relationships by encouraging or discouraging human contact.

Space

The distance we keep between ourselves and others has been the focus of research by psychologists, sociologists, designers, architects, and urban planners. The scientific study of space is called proxemics. Man's concern for space and spatial relations seems to spring from the animal awareness of territory. Territoriality refers to the way in which territory is characteristically taken and defended (Hall, 1959). We think of territory as referring to a place, a spot—acreage or a chair. You probably have places in your own home, apartment, or dorm room that are your places (do you sit in the same seat in class, even though there is no seating chart?).

But, there is also territory around the self, territory that travels with you. This territory has been called "personal space," and acts like an invisible bubble around each of us. When we stay outside the other person's bubble, we are not as intimately involved with the other as when we permit our bubbles (our personal spaces) to overlap (Hall, 1969). The concept of involvement forms a key for understanding much of the observation and research which examines the human use of space.

Four distance zones have been identified from observing middle-class American adults:

intimate distance (0–18 inches) Physical contact and involvement between people is easy. Lovemaking and comforting another occur in this distance zone. All senses can be brought to bear in such physical proximity. Vocalization is probably not necessary, since even a whisper can increase the "psychological" distance between participants.

personal distance (18 inches – four feet) The invisible bubble of space which each of us carries makes up the "close phase," from 18 to 30 inches. The "far phase," from 30 inches to four feet, is just out of reach, although people can touch if both extend their arms. Personal subjects and topics of mutual involvement ususally are discussed at this distance.

social distance (4–12 feet) This space is beyond the limits of involvement with the other person. Small details of the face and body tones cannot be observed. The sense of smell decreases in importance (except in extreme cases, like heavy perfume or non-bathing) and participants cannot easily touch each other. Impersonal topics make up the content of conversation, or formal business may be conducted. Contact can be made and dissolved easily at this distance, i.e., reading the paper at the kitchen table, while your wife fixes dinner.

public distance (12 feet and further) This space is well outside the area of involvement with another person. Only seeing and hearing senses come into play for interaction. In order to be heard, the participants must speak up. The topics of conversation are impersonal and formal, usually planned in advance of speaking.
(Hall, 1969)

In the interpersonal setting, intimate and personal space are our concern. The situation and the relationship suggest appropriate distances. For example, people stand and sit closer to people they like than to people they don't like. We "lean to" another person when we're particularly interested in him (Swenson, 1973). The decrease in distance between us (and the consequent increase in immediacy) provides clues to the liking we have for each other. In a sense, by permitting proximity, we invite contact and involvement with another person. If we observe closeness in others, we infer that they have a liking relationship and treat them accordingly. When one party misuses the space between us by increasing or decreasing it in a manner we consider inappropriate to the social situation, discomfort will follow. A recent study discovered that whites prefer more space between them than do blacks (*Psychology Today,* May 1974). Blacks feel comfortable in conversation in the range of 21 to 24 inches; whites report feeling comfortable with distances of 26 to 28 inches. The subcultural context in which we've learned leads us to interpret proximity differently. "The black moving in close during a conversation may look aggressive or rude to his white companion; while the white backing away looks cold and stand-offish to the black" (*Psychology Today,* May 1974, p. 102).

Working from the notion that discomfort occurs when personal space is invaded, Psychiatrist A. F. Kinzel studied the tolerable distances of prisoners in a federal penitentiary. He found nonviolent men could tolerate invasion up to 18 inches with the distance around the person being nearly cylindrical. For violent men, the comfortable distance was 34 inches from the front and 42 inches from the rear (*Time,* 1969). Approach from the rear was perceived by inmates as particularly menacing.

The personal-space bubble exists, and it may provide us with a clue to understanding criminal violence. The point is that proximity can serve to provide information on liking.

Closeness can provide cues also to dominance within a relationship or a group. The higher-status person in our culture has more right to decrease distance by sitting closer to a lesser-status person than vice-versa (Mehrabian, 1971). We Americans tend to give the more dominant person in a relationship more space. In many homes there is "dad's den" or "dad's workroom," which is not to be invaded by the children. In a sense, the high-status person in a relationship has access to more locations in space (those of the lower-status person which he may invade and his own which may not be invaded by the lower-status person) and the right to increase or decrease immediacy (Mehrabian, 1971).

Another spatial way in which the higher-status person may dominate the relationship is to change the proximity between the participants, which may initiate or terminate a conversation (Hinde, 1972). I have found it okay to say "Hi" to students unknown to me, and they respond to me. Some even say "Hi" first. But, I can't recall a student unknown to me ever to strike up a conversation with me, particularly if I was wearing my coat-and-tie uniform.

Another aspect of status, as it demonstrates the use of space, can be found in the concept of group leadership. In our culture, people at the head of the table are considered "leader." People who consider themselves leaders in a small group tend to gravitate to the head of the table (Abarbanel, 1972). I guess if you want to have influence in a group or be considered leader, you ought to put yourself in the chair at the head of the table.

Physical Appearance

Fortunately for some, and unfortunately for the majority of us, personal relationships can be encouraged or discouraged by our physical appearance, including our body type and the way in which we dress ourselves. Research on the body has found consistently that the physical attractiveness of the other person is an important variable in interpersonal attraction (Byrne et al.,

82

1968). Apparently, in our culture, physical appeal is a positive value. We want to feel attractive, date attractive people, marry them and have attractive children (Byrne et al., 1968). How attractive we are perceived to be, and whom we perceive to be attractive, partially determine with whom we will form closer relationships.

Interestingly, Birdwhistell (Davis, 1972) asserts beauty/ugliness and grace/awkwardness can be learned: The culture can shape these characteristics by reinforcing the individual's behavior. He suggests that we learn to hold our facial features in various ways which can make us appear attractive or ugly. How we hold and pose the body is also learned behavior and contributes to our attractiveness (Davis, 1972). The "strut" of some young black males, through its gait, rhythms, and emphasis on sexual parts of the body, is a learned behavior, designed to enhance attractiveness (Johnson, 1971).

Fortunately, the physical attributes considered attractive within our culture, change—"thin is in," "the natural look," "the athletic look." Certainly, preferences for body types have changed—endomorphs were preferred in the 19th Century, ectomorphs in the sixties, and the mesomorph in the twenties and today. Let's briefly describe each body type and identify several cultural sterotypes.

The *endomorph body type* tends toward softness, roundness of shape and fat. People consider the *ectomorph body type* to be the opposite of the endomorph, tending to be angualr and thin with sharp features. The *mesomorph body type* is thought of as muscular, athletic, big-boned.

Each of these body types encourages cultural stereotyping by people in interpersonal situations. The endomorph is rated: fatter, older, shorter, more old-fashioned, lazier, less strong (physically), less good-looking, more good-natured and agreeable, more dependent on others, and more trusting of others (Wells and Siegel, 1961). Notice the perception of "less good-looking." If physical attractiveness is considered of critical importance in interpersonal preferences, an endomorph may be at a disadvantage in establishing interpersonal relationships. But, it is also possible that the other endomorph stereotyped characteristics (like good-natured, agreeable, more trusting) may compensate for lack of attractiveness, so that relationships can be built. We're not saying that endomorphs are unattractive. We are reporting the research that identified the stereotyped characteristics of endomorphs in our culture.

The ectomorph is rated: thinner, younger, more ambitious, taller, more suspicious of others, more tense and nervous, less masculine, more stubborn and more inclined to be difficult, more pessimistic and quieter.

Finally, the mesomorph body type is rated: stronger, more masculine, better-looking, more adventurous, younger, taller, more mature, and more self-reliant. Whether correct or not, apparently stereotypes exist which connect body type to personal temperament. The presence of physical stereotypes may make initial contact between people more difficult for some than for others. Since we can all think of examples of happy people living relationally full lives, the stereotyping within our culture does not determine doom for some. But, the stereotypes may slow the process of getting together.

Certainly, how we feel about ourselves will affect our contacts with others. The body seems important in this regard. Body image has been reported as related to self-esteem, and it seems to carry over into other areas of personality which affect human contact. People who have above-average body images also consider themselves "more likeable, assertive, conscientious and even more intelligent than the 'average person' " (*Psychology Today*, November, 1973, p. 126). In this particular questionnaire, nearly 79 percent of the people who reported above-average body images also indicated they were more likeable than the average person. Of course, just because they thought they were more likeable, doesn't mean others perceived them that way. Nonetheless, as mentioned in the self-concept chapter, how people perceive themselves does affect how they behave toward others and how they expect others to behave toward them.

Dress

We can influence others' perceptions of us by the clothes we wear (Dowling, 1972). Clothes are used to create images of who we are and how we feel about ourselves. Although we don't know much about how clothing affects our ability to communicate with others, there are some interesting conclusions made in research literature. Clothing does seem to make a difference when making judgments about strangers (Knapp, 1972), but not much difference when judging acquaintances. Initial impressions and the initial willingness to interact with another are affected by the clothes we wear. This seems to indicate that once we know another person, the clothes he wears, which display his moods and his self-concept, don't have much affect on us.

On initial meetings clothes help us place another person within categories—stereotypes, again, if you will. While we might not wish to admit stereotyping another by his clothes, such decisions do help us determine how we behave toward him. Eventually, we'll learn to deal with him on other levels, but initially . . .

Do people act upon stereotypes based on clothing? Yes. In a study of 206 subjects using phone booths, the experimenter asked confederates to dress as high-status and low-status persons. High-status males wore suits and ties; low-status males wore work clothes and carried an object to indicate they were workers. High-status women confederates wore neat dresses and wore or carried coats; low-status women wore inexpensive skirts and blouses and were generally unkempt. A dime was left in the phone booth. After an unsuspecting caller entered the booth, the confederate approached and said he thought he'd left a dime in the booth and asked the caller if he'd found it. Seventy-seven percent of the callers encountering the high-status-dressed confederate returned the dime; only 38 percent returned the money to the low-status-dressed confederate (Bickman, 1974). In public speaking, where the establishment of speaker credibility is so important, the selection of clothes may be a critical strategy. That is, people initially respond to others based on stereotypes prompted by the clothing worn. So, when facing a new audience, a speaker needs to carefully choose what to wear in order to enhance his status.

A similar experiment looked at the way in which people respond to directives from others dressed as low-authority (sports jacket and tie), little-authority (milkman uniform), and high-authority (policeman uniform, albeit a security guard) figures. One of the situations for observation had a confederate standing by a car and parking meter with the authority figure asking a pedestrian to give the confederate a dime for the meter. The people, old and young, men and women, were more obedient to the high-authority guard than to the other two figures (Bickman, 1974).

From this brief discussion of physical appearance and dress, we may conclude that "in a brief encounter, the first thing most people notice is the sex, age, race and physical appearance, including clothes of the other person. These may seem superficial qualities, but they are important determinants of one person's reaction to another" (Bickman, 1974, p. 49).

Body Movements

The movements of the body (postures, orientation, gestures, head movements) have probably received the greatest amount of nonverbal research attention, excepting the face.

Obviously, some of these orientations encourage interaction. Sitting face-to-face is more likely to get people "into it" than sitting back-to-back. Yet, studied separately, body orientation does not seem to make much difference interpersonally. One reason may be that more than 1,000 human postures have been identified. Another reason may be that eye contact confounds research results. Certain body orientations permit greater eye contact, and the more uninviting positions can be overcome by turning the head to permit eye contact (Mehrabian, 1969). One variable important to us as communicators is the degree of body orientation, the degree to which the axis of our bodies (identified by our shoulder position) is turned from and/or to others. Hall conceptualized body orientation into nine major positions (Hall, 1966). (There are, of course, intermediate variations of each.)

The social situation also seems to have some effect on shoulder orientation. When participating in a cooperative activity, people tend to sit side-by-side. When competing, as in bargaining, people tend to sit face-to-face (Hinde, 1972). This difference in situations may be due also to the amount of eye contact available. Perhaps when competing, people want to

86

"see what the other guy is doing" and so, sit head-on. Apparently, body orientation has importance in the communication process. Exactly what importance we're not sure, yet.

The relaxation of the body is another indicator of attitude and status. In the presence of a higher-status individual, people seem to sit more erect. If interested in or liking the other person, we tend to lean toward him/her. Relaxing the posture when sitting generally moves the body away from the other. So, striking a more relaxed position may signal less positive attitudes toward the speaker, in the same way that increasing distance between interactants reflects a negative attitude.

Gestures, like posture, have generated inconsistent results in observation and research. Of course, certain gestures stimulate fairly consistent interpretations across observers within a given social situation: the V with the fingers; the clenched fist; the pointing index finger; an outstretched arm with hand turned upward; fingers close together and palm toward the observer. If any one gesture fails to convey consistent interpretations, frequency of gesturing does. We tend to think of increased body activity as an indication of emotional arousal; we tend to think of decreased activity of the hands and head as an indication of a depressed mood (Knapp, 1972). Perhaps some of the difficulty in interpreting any particular hand gesture is the tremendous amount of movement potential—more than 5,000 different hand gestures have been identified (Krout, 1954).

Gestures are used as "markers" for the interaction between people (Schleflen, 1964). Turning the hand outward (with palm up) to our conversation participant may signal that it's his turn to speak. Tilting the head between sentences may indicate a transition; clasping the hands together and relaxing them back toward the self may signal, "I am done speaking—it is your turn." Gestures are important in human interaction, then, as: (a) substitutes for language, (b) indicators of emotional intensity and general mood, and (c) punctuation marks for conversation.

Body Rhythms

A new area of research that has crept into nonverbal communication literature is body rhythms. While we have been

87

concerned about rhythms governing our lives (i.e., the circadian rhythm determining when we are active and when we sleep), only in the past few years have we begun to discover how rhythms can affect our willingness and ability to communicate with others. An important rhythm is the menstrual cycle. Evidence has been accumulated to verify what many a female has known since puberty—women undergo changes in moods and actions during the menstrual cycle (Bardwick, 1971). Many feel most optimistic and competent at mid-cycle (ovulation) and depressed, hostile, and even anxious just before or during actual menstruation (Paige, 1973). Certainly, changes of this kind, coupled with her physical discomfort, can affect how the woman relates to others. It is interesting to note that cycles similar to menstruation have been found in men. Results of observation in industry found the male cycle affected the way in which men interacted with their co-workers (Luce, 1971).

Some European researchers claim to have identified three biorhythms existing in men and women:

sensitivity rhythm roughly corresponds to the 28-day menstrual cycle. This cycle represents our sensitivity, our emotions, nerves, feelings, cheerfulness, and creativity. It is sometimes called the feminine rhythm.

physical rhythm follows a 23-day cycle. This cycle represents physical strength, endurance, energy, resistance, and confidence. It is sometimes called the masculine rhythm.

intellectual rhythm follows a 33-day cycle. It represents the intelligence, memory, mental alertness, logic, and judgment. (Lewis, 1971)

These rhythms can be charted for every individual, beginning with birth. Half of the time, the individual is in an upswing in the cycle; the other half is spent in a downturn. When you are in an upswing in a particular cycle, you will exhibit attributes represented by the cycle. For instance, Billie Jean King was reported to be in a high phase on the intellectual sensitivity rhythms when she beat Bobby Riggs (Naunton, 1974). Of course, since the cycles do not follow the same pattern, you might be having a "high" in intellectual activity while being "down" a bit emotionally. One researcher of biorhythms reports that Mark Spitz won his Olympic gold medals when the physical and sensitivity curves were synchronized in the positive. His intellectual was down, according to Researcher Harold Willis, but was considered of little significance in his swimming achievement (Naunton, 1974).

Critical days are those where the cycle passes the mid-point between high and low. These can be particularly difficult days. A Tokyo taxi firm has made good use of this knowledge: it has cut its accident rate by 60 percent by cautioning its drivers to be extra careful on their critical days.

We are a long way from understanding the rhythms that seem to affect our lives. But, there seems to be some relationship between our biorhythms and our interpersonal behaviors, if only in making us more willing and capable of engaging in interaction with others during particular periods. The same overall generalization can be made of physical behavior of the body.

Face and Eyes

The face is considered to be the primary source of information about the emotional states of people. The face reflects attitudes toward objects and people. When we want feedback from others, we look to the face. When we want to know how the other feels or what he's thinking, we look to the face. What gives the face this importance in human communication is the ability of the facial muscles to change the face's appearance.

The face contains three relatively independent regions: the brows and forehead; the eye area; and the lower face, including the mouth. Make faces, watching yourself in the mirror. Notice that you can move the brows without moving the mouth region. Eyes can be opened, half-closed, closed and squeezed tightly shut without affecting the rest of the face. The human facial structure permits the face to create more than 1,000 different expressions (Ekman and Friesen, 1971), but we use only a few words to describe these actions: i.e., smile, frown, grin, squint, all describe facial expressions for which there are scores of fine gradations in muscular movement.

Considerable research has been undertaken to understand

emotional display, particularly because of the face's potential to provide information about the emotional state of the individual. One research trend, begun by Ekman and Friesen, shows that certain facial expressions of emotion can be correctly identified cross-culturally. Most nonverbal research maintains that non-verbal behavior and its interpretations are learned. Ekman and Friesen (1971) don't dispute that conclusion, but they do suggest that there may be some universal facial behaviors which (because of the muscle structure) become common and interpretable by people in different cultures. They have studied people's responses to facial expressions in the U.S., Japan, Chile, Argentina, preliterate cultures with minimal Western contact, and isolated preliterates in the southeast highlands of New Guinea (Ekman and Friesen, 1971).

Seven "universal" facial expressions emerged from their research:

happiness	surprise
sadness	disgust
anger	fear

interest

Other emotions displayed by the face may be considered blends of these basic seven. However, accurate interpretation of the face—including the "universals" presented here—seems to require awareness of what evoked the emotion, and the social situation in which the emotion is expressed (Ekman and Friesen, 1969). In other words, we look to the face for information. But, to interpret what the facial expressions mean, we need to know what stimulated the expression, and the social situation in which the expression was made.

Because the face is so important to us, we tend to monitor our own faces, studying what they are doing in a relatively objective manner. Because of this monitoring, we are able also to deceive others more readily with our faces, by concealing our emotions, or visually creating them, where viscerally they do not exist (Ekman and Friesen, 1969). Even "smiling" has been found to be difficult to interpret (Birdwhistell, 1970). Thinking that smiling expressed pleasure in any culture, Birdwhistell found contradictions in giving and interpreting smiles. He found that middle-class people from Ohio, Indiana, and Illinois smiled much more than did individuals with comparable backgrounds from New England. People from Atlanta, Louisville, Memphis, and Nashville smiled even more. (I would, too, if I lived in a warm climate!) Further, it was found that smiling could indicate pleasure, humor, ridicule, doubt, acceptance, and whether an insult was intended or denied. In England, Dr. Michael Chance also studied smiles and found that if the observer lacked knowledge of other facial movements (particularly the eyes), then "smiles would not really mean what they seem" (*Time*, 1969). So, while the three separate areas of the face can move independently, they work together to generate meaning in the observer.

The mouth region is particularly important in generating facial expression when we speak. The movement of the mouth to make speech changes the expression. Further attention is drawn to the mouth because that region is the outlet for the words.

However, the eyes are the major source of interpersonal information. They continually scan the environment, stopping on objects or events for from .25 to .35 seconds (Argyle, 1967). If we become interested in something in the environment (i.e., when talking with another person), we may look at him/her for periods of one to ten seconds. Two persons usually look at each other during the conversation from 25 to 75 percent of the time. During the conversation, about 30 percent of the time will be spent in mutually looking—eye contact. Our culture believes that looking at another person indicates heightened interest in the other—either liking, including sexual interest, or aggressiveness (Argyle, 1967). If both persons look at each other, the heightened interest suggests a willingness to be involved with each other—an important ingredient in building relationships. One reason public speakers attempt to maintain eye contact with the audience is to keep them involved with the speech.

Involvement with the other can be signalled in another way by the eyes. The pupils themselves may signal interest in and liking for what is being seen. When we see someone we like, our pupils automatically expand; when we do not like someone, our pupils contract (*Family Weekly*, 1971). One study suggests that

91

pupil dilation (enlargement) may influence liking choices without the chooser being consciously aware of the subject's pupils. People were asked to choose between two partners—one who would be pleasant, trusting and easy to talk with. The overwhelming choice was the partner whose eyes had been dilated by the experimenter, although the chooser did not know this. Eye contact was given as the reason, but both partners emitted the same amount, and no one mentioned the size of the pupils (Knapp, 1972).

The direction in which we look in conversation has been found to be an indicator of personality. When asked a question, people consistently will look away in the same direction—extroverts to the right; introverts to the left. This tendency was also found in congenitally blind people and had no relationship with being right- or left-handed (*Family Weekly*, 1971). Some recent research suggests this looking pattern may be a function of hemisphere dominance in the brain—if left dominant, one looks right and vice-versa.

We can draw several conclusions about eye behavior, particularly as it relates to interpersonal interaction:

1. Whites look more while listening than while talking; blacks reverse the pattern.

2. People are motivated to look at another to:

   a. gain feedback about what they have been saying

   b. express interest in the other person (mutual looking suggests reciprocal involvement in the other)

   c. cue the other person that it is his turn to speak

   d. express dominance in the situation
   (*Time*, 1969)

Even with these conclusions, we are left with the same problem we've identified with the other nonverbal cues: interpretation appears determined by the social situation, by previously experienced behavior from earlier encounters, and by our awareness of the other person.

Touch

Touch is a powerful nonverbal cue when it comes to inter-personal relationships, yet it is often neglected in our society. Much has been written about touch, but usually from an observational point of view. We have little "hard data" from which to draw conclusions. The study of touch includes being touched (being tactilely stimulated) and touching (the intentional reaching out to make contact). Recent psychological therapeutic efforts have been directed to increasing the touching and being touched behavior of people in our culture.

Being touched (beginning with tactile stimulation inside the womb) may be the first sensory experience for the child. Birth itself provides the infant with considerable stimulation through the skin, culminating with the slap that starts the breathing. During infancy, the baby has need for touch. Children who are denied touch are slower to develop language than children who are not denied touch. Further, the infrequently-touched child develops an affection-hunger which manifests itself in a desire to give and receive sexual touching (Montagu, 1971). By being touched, cuddled, caressed and stroked, the child learns he is loved and wanted—an important beginning in the development of self-esteem.

For men, deprivation of touch in childhood can carry over into an inability to love, even in a sexual sense. As the child grows, the mother decreases the amount of touching so the young boy won't develop an over-dependence upon her. Father withdraws so his boy won't become a homosexual. As a result, the lack of tactile stimulation may prevent the boy-child from developing tender, gentle ways of expressing his love for another. The result may be a rushing of the sexual act, a lack of gentleness with his sexual partner, and insufficient touching during foreplay and intercourse. The lack can bring a reduction in pleasure for the woman, who finds the act rushed, coarse, and void of the cuddling and caressing actions of lovemaking (Montague, 1971).

Touch is interpersonally powerful because to be touched requires an invasion of one's personal space, the space we use to protect ourselves from others. The permission of invasion it-

93

self becomes a "giving" to the other person. Touching is powerful also because each participant is mutually stimulated. I feel your hands, their wetness and their heat upon my shoulders, while you feel my skin, its warmth and its malleability as it moves in your hands.

Touch can serve also as a regulator of interaction. When you're talking, and you momentarily stop to gather your thoughts or breath, haven't you ever reached out and touched your partner on the arm because you thought he was going to speak? In essence, you are "holding him back" from speaking until you are finished.

It is touch as an expression of loving that is most important to all of us. Love to a child, love to a friend, or love to a lover, touch is an expression of love that requires mutual involvement.

INFORMATION PROVIDED BY NONVERBAL BEHAVIOR

The nonverbal portions of messages provide us with information concerning (a) the intended interpretation of the verbal message; (b) the emotional state of the sender; and (c) the state of the relationship between sender and receiver.

Interpretation of the Verbal

The nonverbal actions of the communication participants clue each other as to how to interpret the content (verbal) aspect of the message. The voice, face, and body all can help us to interpret the message of others. Sometimes, the sender intentionally performs certain nonverbal behaviors to enhance our understanding. For example, people come into my office and say:

"THIS is an OFFICE!" with a wide mouth, expressing surprise and wonder, and the voice volume higher than normal.

"This is an office?" with a wide mouth, expressing surprise, and voice volume normal but the tone rising at the end of the sentence.

"THIS is an office!?!" with the mouth curled in disgust, the voice volume higher than normal, and the tone rising at the end of the sentence.

In all these cases, the speaker clued me as to how to interpret his verbal message. The first was a colleague from another department, who· was amazed by the size of my office. The second was a student's parent, who was amazed at the informality. The third was my department chairman, who was disgusted by the clutter. The vocal qualities of tone, rate, rhythm, etc., are called paralanguage.

Often we receive unintentional cues as to how to interpret the message. A raised eyebrow, a curl of the lip, and slow sipping are all cues that "This is a good drink" might not be a sincere compliment, but rather a "nice" statement.

As we mentioned earlier, the nonverbal can repeat, substitute, accent, regulate, contradict, and reflect the sender's feelings about the message in order to assist the receiver in assigning meaning to the verbal message. Ultimately, how I interpret the message will be a function of the relationship between us. The consequence of the development of a relationship is the creation of a set of rules which govern that relationship. What topics we speak freely about, what topics we avoid, who dominates and in what situations, and the depth of involvement, all are governed by an implicit set of rules for the relationship.

Emotional State

When we look at the movements, facial expressions, or muscle tone of another person, we are able to infer an emotional state: anger, happiness, surprise, fear, interest, sadness, or disgust. Nonverbal cues originate in the body (Goldenson, 1970), and emotions cause changes in the body observed in bodily reactions. Therefore it doesn't surprise us that we acquire emotional information from the nonverbal portion of a message. These behavioral manifestations, which can be perceived and interpreted by observers, we classify as nonverbal information—information which can assist us in creating a communication-state. Many of these behaviors may not be intended, may even be unconsciously emitted. But, once perceived and interpreted, these unintentional behaviors become part of the total message. The actions of the body, then, provide us with information about the emotional state of the individual.

The face provides us with the greatest amount of information about the person's emotional state (Duncan, 1969). The face has almost constant visibility in interpersonal situations. The body hides under clothing; hands may be stuffed into pockets; but, the face remains continually available for inspection by the observer and may be considered the best single indicator of the individual's emotional state.

If the face is the best indicator of the emotional state (often referred to as affect display in the research literature), then the body provides the best measure of emotional intensity (Ekman and Friesen, 1969). Muscle tone, speed of movements, voice tone and volume, posture, eye blinking, all provide the observer with cues as to the strength of the feeling or emotion being displayed. The tightly clenched fists, bulging muscles, and erect stance with feet wide apart of the father, whose youngest son just "painted" the family car, probably tells us that ol' dad is mighty upset! Clenched and shaking fists tell us plenty. So do kicking, running, and slouching. What is meant is this: if you have to choose the part of the body that most often tells us the emotional state, choose the face. If you know the general emotional state, then the rest of the body provides clues to the intensity of that feeling.

State of the Relationship

The nonverbal actions of the communication participants clue each of them to the relationship between them: the degree of liking that exists; who, if either, is dominant; the extent of the involvement of each in the other, are all transmitted nonverbally. These three aspects have been described as dimensions of human feeling and attitudes in human relationships by Mehrabian in his book, *Silent Messages*. Liking (dimension of immediacy), status (dimension of power), and involvement with the other (dimension of responsiveness) are seen as dimensions of an interpersonal relationship, about which nonverbal behavior provides information. Let's look at each dimension to see what can be communicated nonverbally about the relationship, and which nonverbal behaviors might exemplify each dimension.

The *immediacy dimension* describes liking-disliking and approach-avoidance in human relationships. We tend to approach what we like and avoid what we do not like. Such information is essential to the development and maintenance of a relationship.

The distance between us provides information about our liking. If I like you and you like me, we probably will stand closer to one another than we would if we did not care for one another (Hinde, 1972). While there may be some cultural differences (Arabs and Latin Americans typically stand closer together than North Americans do), the interpersonal distance between people is related to the comparative physical distance between them. There are ways to increase, or decrease the distance between us, without changing the measurable space separating us. I can lean toward you to decrease our separation. Or, the psychological distance between us can be reduced by engaging in greater eye contact. Decreasing eye contact, looking away, and leaning backward can increase the separation. Changes in the distance between participants can indicate that one wishes to begin or end the interaction (Hinde, 1972). Touch (the intentional reaching out to someone) also decreases the distance between participants. What is important here is that nonverbal cues can tell an observer the degree of liking you have for him.

The *power dimension* describes the dominance in a relationship. Who has the greatest status? Who dominates the relationship within the particular setting? One consistent indicant of perceived status within a relationship has been the degree of body relaxation. The more relaxed person indicates the one with the higher status (Mehrabian, 1971). The higher-status person typically can exhibit more relaxed behaviors, like leaning backward in his chair, slouching, casual manner and dress, while the lower-status person is generally less relaxed. For example, a committee assignment required that I interview the university president. During the course of our interview, I became increasingly amused by my own behavior. I wore a coat and tie to the president's office, when slacks and sweater are my usual attire. I waited to be seated until invited to do so. I sat with my feet flat on the floor, when usually I sprawl in my classes or my office. I sat directly facing him. The president wore a shirt and tie under a pullover sweater. He sat sprawled out in his chair, put his feet on his desk, talked to the wall as much as to me, and gestured freely and often. I rigidly held my notebook. Even though I knew what was happening, I could not bring myself to adopt the air of informality the president was able to assume.

But, the higher-status person can do more than relax. Part of higher status is the right to initiate intimacy. Usually, the higher-status person initiates the contact—the executive invites the secretary to lunch; the foreman shares a beer with an assembly-line worker; a professor invites a student out for coffee. Initiating touch is also the prerogative of the higher-status person. Many times, I've watched a certain bank president place his hand on the shoulder of a subordinate, implying an interpersonal "closeness." Never have I seen a subordinate imply this same intimacy by either initiating touch by placing a hand on that bank president's shoulder or reciprocating his move.

Information about the status of the two or more people within the relationship is provided by the nonverbal cues given off by each participant.

The *responsive dimension* describes the degree of involvement each participant has with the other. "Responsiveness refers to the extent of awareness and the reaction to another" (Mehrabian, 1971, p. v). To be aware and reactive to another suggests an involvement. To be nonreactive suggests a lack of involvement. Responsiveness may be determined by observing the intensity and amount of response toward another individual that takes place over time. When you are near, I look at you, I smile often, wink perhaps, and seem "vital" in my physical movements. We would say I am responding to you.

Two of the three kinds of information conveyed nonverbally are intertwined: the state of the relationship (immediacy, power, and responsiveness) and the interpretation of the verbal. The state of the relationship affects how I interpret the message, and the interpretation of the verbal message affects the kind of relationship we build. We separate them only to be able to talk about them.

Nonverbal behavior provides the communication participants with information about how to interpret the verbal messages, the emotional states of each other, and the relationship between them.

WAYS TO OVERCOME THE MYTH

1. Be cautious in the assignment of meaning to the actions of others. Remember that every little action does not have a meaning all its own. As is true of assigning meaning to language, the meaning for any physical or environmental cue comes from within the observer.

2. Look for patterns of behavior in others within separate environments. Watch the eyes, facial expressions, posture, gestures, and dress of other people as they move and talk within different social settings: i.e., in the dorm, in the classroom, at work, at home with their family, with friends of the same or opposite sex.

a. Make a journal of observations of a person who is important to you. Keep the journal for a two-week period. Establish four times during a 24 hour day that you usually can observe the person. Select times which reflect different activities: i.e., 7:30 a.m. with the family; 10:30 a.m. at the office (class, coffee klatch, etc.); 5:30 p.m. at home; 9:30 p.m. with the family (or close friends). Enter in the journal descriptions of the activities, including the topics discussed, and the physical behavior of the person. How do they sit? What is their body orientation? gestures? eye contact? touching? physical appearance? At the end of the two-week period, examine the journal to find patterns of behavior. Can you find consistent collections of behavior when the person is happy? angry? distressed? hassled? Write a description of these patterns. Now, show the person what you've done, your observations and conclusions. Discuss the patterns and how they seem to affect the interpersonal interaction of the person.

b. Have a person important to you keep a journal of your behavior. Such record keeping may help you to identify patterns of behaving that may be confusing to others; so confusing that what you want to get across is not coming through because some other physical or environmental cue you may not be aware of dominates.

3. Interview people to see how the environment affects interpersonal contacts. Using a dormitory floor, a city block, a department of a business, interview the people to find with whom they have the greatest and the least contact. You can do this by having the interviewee list names of people he contacts, or select from a list of names you provide. Using a map of the environment, match the most and least contacted person with his/her position in the drawing, i.e., are the names of people in the middle of the block most often mentioned by the neighbors? the residents closest to the stairs in the dorm? the desk nearest the drinking fountain in the office? By developing a greater awareness of the influence of the environment upon your interpersonal contacts, you may be sensitive to how you position yourself within any social setting.

4. Following a careful analysis of your own behavioral patterns within social settings, change those patterns. For example, if you usually maintain eye contact with people when you talk to them, don't! If you have felt discomfort in maintaining eye contact with people, work hard to overcome your discomfort and do it! If you talk with students or subordinates from behind your desk, come around to the front. Your objective is to break the pattern of behavior in order to observe the impact and influence your nonverbal behavior has upon the people around you. Once you've observed the impact, you will be in a position to more carefully monitor your own behavior in the future.

5. Work to be consistent in the verbal and nonverbal messages you send. This requires that you discover the potential of your own body as a message sender and that you discover the messages that your body wants to send. Discover what you are feeling and permit your body to express that emotion. For men this is particularly important for in our culture we tend to discourage men from expressing emotion. One result of this limitation is a decreased ability to read the nonverbal cues of others. Another result is the male effort to hide the "true" emotion which creates bodily actions of discordance and confusion for the observer.

6. Create a public speech in which you research a nonverbal cue of people from another culture or subculture; i.e., facial expressions, use of space and time, postures, gestures, and eye contact. Attempt to relate the nonverbal cues used in other cultures to your own. By developing a greater awareness of how other cultures behave, you may develop a greater awareness of yourself, how important nonverbal behavior is, how it is learned and the differences in interaction patterns between peoples.

SUMMARY

A myth exists in our society which suggests that every movement has meaning unto itself. We've tried to dispel that belief by first identifying the problems of interpreting nonverbal behavior: (a) nonverbal behavior is learned; (b) nonverbal behavior is bound by social context; (c) nonverbal behavior is not readily translated into language.

Then we looked at the ways in which nonverbal cues work with the verbal to create total messages. They help us repeat, substitute, accent, reflect the sender's feelings about the message, reflect changes in environment, regulate the transactions, and contradict the verbal message.

Next, we looked at research findings which demonstrate some culturally consistent meanings. The areas presented were environment, space, physical appearance and dress, body movements, body rhythms, face and eyes, and touch.

We examined what people seem to learn from nonverbal messages. We saw what people do not learn (at least not as well) in the verbal. We looked at the factors involved in these processes: the interpretation of the verbal message, the emotional states of others, and the state of the relationship between interactants, i.e., the extent of their liking, their status, and the involvement between them. We have also suggested ways to overcome the myth about nonverbal communication.

5

SELF-CONCEPT

MYTH
"I Don't Need Nobody!"

A counselor friend of mine says that one of the greatest problems articulated to him by college students is loneliness. "Nobody likes me. I have no friends." The counselor often asks if the student has made the effort to make contact with other students, or members of the faculty, or members of the community. The answer is often, "Yes, but after a little while we just drift apart." The next question he usually asks is, "Did you let these people get to know you? Did you tell them how you felt about things? about them? about experiences you were having together?

"No," is the frequent reply. "If I told them those kinds of things, they might find out what I'm really like. If they got to know me, they might not like me." People who feel this way remain lonely. They believe the myth.

Statements like those of the student, manifest the belief that we are who we are as individuals, independent of others. Somehow, I am who I am, because I am: who you are, and how you respond to *me* and to *us,* has nothing to do with my development as an individual. Some may believe in independence of humans within a social environment. Others may believe because of a religious doctrine, which may suggest that all men are born with a predetermined kernel of self hidden deep within them.

Such a doctrine sees life as a commitment to the discovery of one's own kernel. But, man is a social being. People we make contact with mold our behaviors. A part of that molding is the development, maintenance, and change in one's self-concept.

SELF-CONCEPT DEFINED

You believe you are an interesting person to talk to, possess better than average intelligence, are a thrower of attractive ceramics, and a friendly, if inept, tennis partner. You have identified beliefs which partially make up your own image of you. This image we call the self-concept. One's self-concept, then, may be thought of as an organized set of beliefs we hold about ourselves.

These beliefs about ourselves include both definitional and evaluative beliefs concerning our physical and intellectual abilities, as well as our ability to sustain interpersonal relationships. Beliefs incorporated into one's self-concept include self-descriptions, statements about who I am, and self-evaluations, statements which judge whether who I am is good or bad. Statements about self which illustrate the former are: I am a college teacher; I am slightly overweight; I am slightly taller than average; I play golf. Some self-evaluative beliefs are: I am a good teacher; I am physically attractive; I am a good golfer.

Real and Ideal Identity

Some of the beliefs we hold about ourselves are not realistic when measured against who we are at any particular moment in time. They are beliefs about what we would *like* to be—our ideal self (Jessor and Feshbach, 1968). Both the present self and the ideal self help to motivate my behavior. Both set ranges for appropriate behavior (including speaking and listening) within social situations. For example, once I think of myself as a college professor, I establish a range of behavior I will exhibit in the classroom. Now, if my ideal self-image suggests that I ought to be a college president, then my appropriate range of behavior is narrowed. It is narrowed to exclude teaching behaviors I see as inappropriate for a college president, i.e., swearing, jeans, sitting on the floor.

SOCIAL FUNCTIONS OF SELF-CONCEPT

Taken together, the sum total of beliefs about myself comprise my self-concept. The self-concept performs two useful social functions: (1) the self-concept sets a base line of expectations for my own behavior, and (2) the self-concept sets a base line of expectations for the behavior of others toward me. The setting of behavioral expectations helps us cope with uncertainty in social situations by providing pre-conceived plans of action. Certain behavioral choices are not open to me because they do not fit the concept I have of myself.

If I did not have this basic set of behavioral expectations, each new social situation would be completely unpredictable. Each new social situation would pose an infinite number of behavioral alternatives, and I would have to make an infinite number of choices. All my intellectual and emotional energies would be diverted to making simple choices of how to behave, instead of being able to focus my energies upon relationships and the subtleties of other's behaviors.

Expectations for my own behavior

Self-definition. The beliefs I hold about myself make up an organized set of statements about who and what I am. Collectively, they place me in a social reality; they define my boundaries for me; they help direct my behaviors. For instance, if I say I am a liberal Republican, then by definition, I am not a socialist, communist, labor-union democrat, or John Bircher. Therefore, I will join some groups while avoiding others.

Or, a middle-aged woman who has borne several children and is self-conscious of stretch scars and a slight tummy bulge (whether attractive or not), may avoid social activities which demand body exposure, i.e., swimming, tennis, racquet ball, golf, etc. Or, a woman who considers herself elegant, sophisticated, and feminine may avoid camping trips with her husband and sons because the "roughing it" and the "pioneer spirit" do not match her self-concept. Self-concept beliefs, then, can inhibit our participation in certain activities by defining our behavioral boundaries.

On the other hand, self-concept beliefs can also encourage our participation in certain activities. The young business-man who considers himself an intelligent, attractive leader will be motivated to participate in activities which confirm that belief. Therefore, we might find him on the board of a country club, in the Chamber of Commerce, involved in fund-raising activities in his community, and developing a scratch handicap golf game.

Base line for my behavior. My self-concept also provides a base line from which I can observe and moderate my own behavior. This base line sets expectations for my behavior in social situations. Once I have developed a concept of who/what I am and how I should relate to others, the concept it-self directs my behavior in future social situations (Fitts, et al., 1971).

For example, not long ago I had a discussion with a senior member of the faculty of our department. He had been teaching the basic speech course for more than fifteen years, under five different course directors. During our conversa-tion, he confided that he had been dubious of many of the recent changes made in the course. One of the changes was the inclusion of more informal activities in which the in-structor took part. He said, "I didn't think I could do that." Then he confessed that he had changed his mind. He found himself able to perform successfully in a less formal class-room environment. His former concept of himself as a col-lege teacher and professor had demanded that there be some aloofness from the students. In other words, that concept of himself as a professor made him suspicious of behaviors which ran counter to his belief of how a college professor should behave in the classroom. Fortunately he tried the new behavior, liked it, and received positive responses from his students. Now, he has changed his teaching techniques in all of his classes and views informal professor-student behavior as appropriate. This new belief has been incorporated into his self-concept and has set new expectations for his relations with students.

The behavioral expectations set by our self-concepts can be both a benefit and a detriment. Sammy Davis, Jr., as portrayed in his autobiography, *Yes, I Can,* provides examples of beneficial expectations. The concept he had of himself, his abilities, his potential, his place in society, suggested that he could conquer racial bias and become whatever he chose.

On the other hand, behavioral expectations can set unnecessary limits on our actions. High school and university classrooms are filled with intelligent students, capable of exploring complicated problems, whose work habits prevent them from effectively attacking tough problems in a systematic way. When you talk with them about why they do not assume additional responsibilities and tackle tough problems, they answer that they would be rejected by their peers if they "set the curve" or "booked too hard." These students believe that they cannot exhibit certain intellectual behaviors because it might make them unacceptable to their peers. They see themselves as part of the group and will not exhibit behavior which deviates from the group's norms. Unwillingness to deviate from norms, even to the denial of self, is not unusual behavior in groups.

Expectations for the Behavior of Others Toward Me

Self-definition. Self-concept beliefs also set our expectations for how we think others should behave toward us. Earlier this semester, a girl asked to see me. She was noticeably upset about having scored the lowest on the first exam. She just couldn't believe that she had done so poorly. Amid tears of frustration, self-anger, and irritation with me came the reason for her concern, "But I'm an 'A' student!" The way in which she had defined herself, "an 'A' student," set expectations for how she would behave and how I, as an instructor, should behave toward her. She should receive an A.

107

Unfortunately, her performance on the first exam did not meet the requirements for an "A." The grade shocked her because she attributed the lack of an "A" to me, and not to her own performance. The point is that self-definitional beliefs establish expectations for how we think others will behave toward us.

INSIGHT 5.1   From *Knots* by R. D. Laing*

My mother loves me.
  I feel good.
I feel good because she loves me.

I am good because I feel good
I feel good because I am good
My mother loves me because I am good.

My mother does not love me.
  I feel bad.
I feel bad because she does not love me
  I am bad because I feel bad
I feel bad because she does not love me
She does not love me because I am bad.

I don't feel good
therefore I am bad
therefore no one loves me.

I feel good
therefore I am good
therefore everyone loves me.

I am good
You do not love me
therefore you are bad. So I do not love you.

I am good
You love me
therefore you are good. So I love you.

I am bad
You love me
therefore you are bad.

* From *Knots,* by R. D. Laing. Copyright © 1970 by The R. D. Laing Trust. Reprinted by permission of Pantheon Books, a Division of Random House, Inc.

Self-evaluation. Our expectations for the behavior of others toward us are also affected by self-evaluational beliefs. If I think "I'm good," then I expect to be treated as "good." When you don't treat me as "good," I'm hurt. I've long considered myself a "good athlete." The belief developed because I could compete successfully in almost all sports. I haven't been a "star" in any sport, but better than most guys in all the sports I've tried. As I have aged, my speed has declined, quickness decreased, and my physical abilities have generally deteriorated. It hurts not to be chosen first when teams are made up, when for years pick-up teams wanted me to play more than other guys. I have always thought of myself as "good." Now, the messages I receive from others say "you're adequate." The point here is that my evaluative beliefs set up expectations for how others should behave to show that they value me.

Self-fulfilling prophecy: An interesting phenomenon when discussing self-concept as it affects my expectations for the other's behavior toward me is called self-fulfilling prophecy (Watzlawick et al., 1967). A person makes an assumption about how others will behave toward him and then acts as if they had already behaved in that way. For example, a girl assumes that she "isn't very smart" (her self-concept includes this self-evaluative belief). In math class, then, she doesn't ask questions, she stops reading textbook assignments, doesn't see the instructor for help, doesn't ask aid from friends, increases her time in the beerhalls. Her teacher begins to see her as lazy, unmotivated, and "not very smart." So, he begins to treat her as "not very smart." When her final grade comes and her parents ask, "why so bad?" she replies, "I'm not very smart." The expectations she set for how others ought to behave toward her encouraged her to behave in the manner she expected them to expect. She prophesied and fulfilled the prophesy. Of course, there can be a positive effect too. In sales trainee programs the potential salesmen are told to "think of yourself as a good salesman and you'll be one."

THE SELF GROWS FROM OTHERS' REACTIONS

Where does the self-concept come from? The self-concept is developed from our experiences with others. We intentionally and unintentionally express parts of ourselves to others— thoughts, feelings, actions—then watch and listen to the way the others respond. In a very real sense, how I look at myself is determined by how others respond to me. I see myself reflected in others' reactions to me. We define ourselves through others.

This conceptualization of self is not new, having been discussed by the sociologist C. H. Cooley in 1912, and stressed in 1934 by the psychologist G. H. Mead. Our relationships with others, the kinds of messages we exchange with them, will affect our self-concepts. The more I interact with someone, the more potential influence he/she has on the development and maintenance of my own self-concept. It is not surprising, then, that the family and other significant people outside the family have a great deal to do with the beliefs we hold about ourselves.

In the Family

When a child is born, he apparently has no concept of self (Mead, 1934). Through tactile exploration, the child begins to discover his physical boundaries—the bottom of his feet, his back, his bottom, the top of his head. Perhaps you have had the delightful experience of being able to watch an infant find his hand for the very first time. You may remember how he carefully explored it with the other hand, staring . . . feeling . . . opening . . . closing . . . twisting. You may even have chuckled as his hand moved out of his field of vision, and he began to search for it, not realizing that it was attached to him. The young child was differentiating—differentiating himself from the environment—through touch and tactile stimulation.

Before long, the child learns that certain actions bring responses of approval and acceptance and/or disapproval and rejection from parents (Bennis, 1968). Cooing brings cuddling, caressing and smiling: wetting his pants causes frowns and unpleasantness.

As the child begins to develop language skills, the concept

110

of self develops more readily. Why? With language, the child can make an object of himself. That is, he can attach language labels to his behavior and then speculate on how this behavior would be received by others, even when other people are not present. It doesn't take many slaps on the bottom for the child to connect "no-no" and "bad boy" with consequences of his own behavior. The self-concept of a child, then, is developed through his exploration of himself, through his observation of reactions of family members to him, and through the objectification of himself with language, which categorizes experience.

Parents may influence the child's self-concept by direct displays of approval and disapproval and also in more subtle ways. In the monograph, *The Self Concept and Self Actualization* (Fitts et al., 1971), the authors report several studies which demonstrate a positive correlation between the self-concept of a child and the self-concepts of his parents. There seems to be some evidence that parents with positive self-concepts tend to have children with positive self-concepts. The parents directly shape the child's self-concept through reactions to the child's behavior—either positive or negative. Parents also indirectly shape the child's self-concept, through modelling. If we want our children to say "please" and "thank you," then we, as parents, need to say "please" and "thank you."

Outside the Family

People outside the home also help the individual to form his self-concept. Peers, schoolteachers, and other adults have important impacts on the development and maintenance of a person's self-concept. When the verbal and nonverbal reactions of people around us confirm our definitional and evaluative beliefs about ourselves and reality, we feel secure and comfortable. When their reactions deny our self-concept, we do not.

The point is that others help mold the beliefs we have about ourselves. They help mold those beliefs by the way in which they react to us.

INSIGHT 5.2   From *Knots* by R. D. Laing*

He can't be happy
        when there is so much suffering in the world
She can't be happy
        if he is unhappy

She wants to be happy
He does not feel entitled to be happy

She wants him to be happy
and he wants her to be happy

He feels guilty if he is happy
and guilty if she is not happy

He wants her to be happy

So they are both unhappy

He accuses her of being selfish
        because she is trying to get him to be happy
        so that she can be happy

She accuses him of being selfish
        because he is only thinking of himself

He thinks he is thinking of the whole cosmos

She thinks she is mainly thinking of him
because she loves him

How can she be happy
when the man she loves is unhappy

He feels she is blackmailing him
by making him feel guilty
because she is unhappy that he is unhappy

She feels he is trying to destroy her love for him
by accusing her of being selfish
when the trouble is
that she can't be so selfish as to be happy
when the man she loves is unhappy

She feels that there must be something wrong with her
to love someone who can be so cruel
as to destroy her love for him
and is too guilty to be happy, and is unhappy because
he is guilty

He feels that he is unhappy because he is guilty
to be happy when others are unhappy and that he made
a mistake to marry someone who can only think of
happiness.

* R. D. Laing, *Knots*, pp. 27–28.

KINDS OF RESPONSES TO SELF-CONCEPT

We can categorize the responses others make to us according to whether the reactions confirm, reject, or disconfirm our conceptions of ourselves. The sentence "Pass the salt" is a directive, asking for action from the receiver. Implicit in the manner in which I say that statement—whether as a demand, a plea, or a quiet request—are hints about the way I see our relationship in this particular situation (Watzlawick et al., 1967). A demand may imply that I see myself as superior to you in our relationship; a plea may indicate that I see myself as subservient to you; a quiet request may suggest that I see you as an equal. The point is that I give clues as to how I see myself in our relationship in every message sent. Of course, how you perceive a statement I make about myself in relationship to you will provide the basis for your reaction to me. Essentially, this reaction will be either a *confirmation, rejection* or *disconfirmation* of my self-concept.

Confirmation

If you accept my definition of self in relationship with you, and you respond in an accepting (positive) manner, you have confirmed my self-concept. Confirmation has been called "the greatest single factor insuring mental development and stability that has so far emerged from our study of communication"

113

(Watzlawick et al., 1967, p. 84). With each confirmation, the confirmed aspect of the self tends to gain in strength. As different aspects of our self-concepts are rewarded within different social situations by different people, these aspects begin to form an integrated identity. We have a decreasing need to search for confirmation from others, a search which diverts our cognitive and emotional energies from other tasks. An integrated identity allows us to respond freely to the social world around us—freely, in the sense that we are not overly concerned with consistency—free to respond as we feel, instead of hiding our feelings. In the case of an integrated identity, the person has a positive self-concept that has been confirmed by a variety of people in a number of different situations, and feels confident in the validity of his self-definition and evaluation (Bennis et al., 1968). If I consider myself to be a leader, and if, in different situations where I am asked to exhibit leadership behavior, those around me reward me by smiling, by thanking me, by electing me to new offices, then the belief about myself as a leader has been confirmed. I can become less concerned with behaving like a leader and become more concerned with being a leader.

INSIGHT 5.3   From *Reaching Out* by David W. Johnson*

A person who has a strong, self-accepting attitude presents the following behavioral picture (Hamachek, 1971):

1.   He believes strongly in certain values and principles and is willing to defend them even in the face of strong group opinion. He feels personally secure enough, however, to modify them if new experience and evidence suggest he is in error.

2.   He is capable of acting on his own best judgment without feeling excessively guilty or regretting his actions if others disapprove of what he has done.

3.   He does not spend undue time worrying about what is coming tomorrow, what has happened in the past, or what is taking place in the present.

4.   He has confidence in his ability to deal with problems, even in the face of failure and setbacks.

5.   He feels equal to others as a person, not superior or inferior, irrespective of the differences in specific abilities, family backgrounds, or attitudes of others toward him.

6.   He is able to take for granted that he is a person of interest and value to others, at least to those with whom he chooses to associate.

7.   He can accept praise, without the pretense of false modesty and compliments without feeling guilty.

8.   He is inclined to resist the efforts of others to dominate him.

9.   He is able to accept the idea and admit to others that he is capable of feeling a wide range of impulses and desires, ranging from being angry to being loving, from being sad to being happy, from feeling deep resentment to feeling deep acceptance.

10.   He is able to genuinely enjoy himself in a wide variety of activities involving work, play, creative self-expression, companionship, or loafing.

11.   He is sensitive to the needs of others, to accepted social customs, and particularly to the idea that he cannot enjoy himself at the expense of others.

* David W. Johnson, *Reaching Out: Interpersonal Effectiveness and Self-Actualization,* © 1972, pp. 144-145. By permission of Prentice-Hall, Inc., Englewood Cliffs, New Jersey.

Rejection

The second category of responses that can be made to my self-concept in relationship to you within a given situation is rejection. In the case of rejection, the other person recognizes the way in which I view the relationship to him and refuses to accept it. Actually, rejection of another's self-concept, even if it sounds harmful, may not be too painful. In fact, the ultimate consequence of rejection may be the development of a more accurate picture of one's self.

For years I was a college debate coach. We tried to recruit the best high school debaters we could. But, coaching the high school "hot-shot" was a problem. He came into our debate program seeing himself as a winner. But, collegiate competition is much more strenuous, the demands for research time and analytical thinking much greater, and the intersquad competition more intense. Often, we had to reject the hot-shot's image of himself in practice sessions in order to prepare him to become a better tournament debater. I can recall a young man practicing a ten-minute speech. With my stopping and starting him in order to offer criticism (*always* in a gentle, smiling fashion!), it took him one hour and 45 minutes to finally deliver an acceptable ten-minute speech. Needless to say, he was hurt. However, a more accurate picture of his abilities emerged. He recognized his need to learn new skills and refine old ones. With the new image of himself, he worked harder, accepted criticism more easily and went on to become a successful participant in national tournaments. In a sense, if we really care for someone we ought to respond negatively (rejection) if the person behaves in a manner we do not like, or see as harmful to him.

Disconfirmation

The third category of responses made to one's self-concept by another within a social situation is disconfirmation. Disconfirmation differs from rejection. Rejection says, "I don't accept what I see you presenting to me, but I do see and understand." To disconfirm another's self-concept suggests that you don't even recognize it; in essence, you're saying to the other, "You do not exist" (Watzlawick et al., 1967). In rejection, we may disagree with another's definition of self and reality. In disconfirmation, we deny the right of the individual to define himself or his reality. I remember riding in a car recently with my wife and a university friend. The friend and I had been talking about problems on the university campus. During a silence, my wife began to comment on the beauties of the rolling, lush countryside and a number of quaint centennial farms we were passing. Practically in mid-sentence, certainly while she was taking a breath, I said to my colleague, "Do you think the changes in federal regulations will help more students get financial aid?" I disconfirmed my wife in this instance. In effect, my statement said to her, "You do not exist; you are not important." This is distinctly different from responding to her by rejecting her message. In rejection, I would simply have disagreed with her, but in disconfirmation, I relegated her to a nonentity. (Digression: my wife is not a weak-willed individual. She informed me quickly and emphatically that I had just exemplified disconfirmation!)

The consequence of frequently receiving disconfirming responses is indeed a loss of self. Why? Because disconfirmation is neither affirmation nor rejection; it is nothing. I don't know where I stand, how others see me, or how others see themselves in relation to me. Parents can harm their children's social development by disconfirming—ignoring requests for attention or affection and efforts of the child to control the situation.

OTHERS AFFECT THE SELF-CONCEPT WHEN ABSENT

Others don't have to be present to affect our self-concepts. We can reflect on past encounters with them in the solitude of our own rooms. Essentially what we do is replay a face-to-face interaction in our minds, trying to remember the reactions made to what we said and what we didn't say. We meditate on those reactions and make some choices and decisions regarding our future behavior.

Besides replaying interaction situations, others can affect our self-concept in their absence by providing examples with which we compare our behavior and beliefs. Festinger (1950) first identified the process he called "social comparison." While Festinger developed a number of hypotheses about the process of social comparison, essentially, it all boils down to this: We appraise and evaluate our behavior by comparing what we do and say with what relevant others do and say. This comparison can be made without the direct presence of those with whom we are comparing ourselves. As a result, the process of developing who we are may be less risky than the direct feedback situation found in face-to-face interactions. The process of social comparison still makes us dependent upon others, though. Obviously, we can't compare our beliefs, our attitudes, our performance without having other people to provide us with examples for comparison. Even though this process of creating an identity, developing a self-image, may be less threatening and less direct, it is still tied to other people.

SELF-CONCEPT, OTHERS AND RELATIONSHIPS

In summing up our discussion of self-concept, we offer three conclusions which relate a person's self-concept to his ability to establish communication-states.

(1) The greater the difference between our self-concept and the concept others have of us, the greater will be the chance for misunderstanding (Myers and Myers, 1973, p. 100). Why? The responses others make to me are not being made to me, but to the me that they see. Since their me is distinctly different from my me, I'm not in a position to accurately interpret the responses they are making: I may see negative reactions as being rewarding, or, I may see rewarding reactions as being negative. A father may be a tough disciplinarian with his son, in the belief that as a father he needs to shape the boy's behaviors and attitudes so he will be prepared for the "hard knocks" of the world. He believes he is being a good father. A neighbor may see such discipline as stifling, arbitrary, and too demanding. The two may be handball partners, but the relationship between them will have a hard time growing, because on the topic of "being a father," the reactions each makes to the other will be misunderstood. They will be misunderstood because their images of "a good father" are considerably different.

(2) The greater the difference between how we see ourselves in the present and how we see our ideal selves, the greater will be the dissatisfaction with our communicative behaviors. In a movie entitled "Journey into Self" (a documentary recording of an encounter group, involving Carl Rogers), there is an excellent example of this conclusion. One weeping Eurasian girl expresses concern for how others have seen her. Since she is diminutive, she has been seen as a "China doll, something tiny

and fragile, which one admires from afar." As the film progresses, she says, "I don't want to be a goddamn China doll ringing a bell. I want to be a real person." The images she carries of herself, what she wants to be, and how she has come to picture herself because of others' reactions to her, are all distinctly different. The difference has led her to dissatisfaction with the way in which she relates to people. In the film she expresses the hope that she can improve her communication skills, so that she can reach out to other people more effectively. The reasons for her wish: she likes other people, she wants to be able to more closely connect the way she looks at herself as a real woman with the way she has come to see herself as a China doll.

(3) The greater the difference between the concepts others have of us and their ideal image of us, the less chance there is for a satisfactory relationship. Part of the dissatisfaction with the relationship will grow because we do not meet each other's expectations. You see me as somewhat less than what I could be. On your part, this may breed irritation toward me—hostility for behavior that you see me emit, which does not match behavior you see for your ideal image of me. Virtually every week, some letter is written to columnist Ann Landers by a wife expressing dissatisfaction with her marriage. Often, the letter says that the wife saw signs of behavior she didn't like in her husband before they were married, but overlooked these faults because she "thought she could change him." The wife wanted a loving husband who would become the Great Provider, a pillar of the community, and who would be worthy of her, but he hasn't measured up. Ann continually advises young singles who express concern about another's behavior to avoid marrying that individual. She takes the attitude, "if a stinker now, a real stinker later." What she is saying is that if the image of the other person does not match your ideal of what that other person ought to be like, then the relationship is not likely to be satisfying.

A final example illustrates the interpersonal and personal difficulties found in our three conclusions. A topless dancer explains that she survives in her job by thinking about other things while she dances. As the music throbs on, she thinks:

"This isn't me, this is not me. Me is not wearing make-up, me is wearing dungarees." (Conclusion No. 2) "I wonder what my neighbors would say. Wow, I don't think there's any way they'd accept it." (Conclusion No. 3) "What I don't like about this job is what people think, people coming into the bar and thinking I'm some kind of an immoral woman or something." (Conclusion No.1) "No sir, that's not me and this is not me."*

How she sees herself, how her customers see her, how her neighbors and children see her (not knowing the truth), and what she'd like to be; the differences cause her discomfort, fear, and a desire to change her life. She wants to leave the city and become a real estate agent.

WE INFLUENCE OTHERS
JUST AS OTHERS INFLUENCE US

We need to remember the other side of the coin as well. If others have profound influence upon us, then we have profound influence upon them. How we react to them and the idealization of them we carry in our heads will affect the quality of our interaction. Such interdependence places great responsibility on each of us for the growth and development of the other. So, in a relationship, a minimum expectation for the behavior of each should be listening and accurate feedback to the other. By accurate, we mean that the verbal and nonverbal messages given off should honestly express the thoughts and feelings experienced at the moment. In this way, each member of the relationship is kept in contact with himself and in contact with the perceptions of the other.

INSIGHT 5.4   Untitled Poem by Marilyn Pees

Looking for oneself is always a
Difficult learning task involving
Discipline and release
Affection and restraint
Faith and courage

---

* *The State Journal,* "Topless Dancer Thinks Other Things on Job," by Mike McGrady from *Newsday,* Sunday, Feb. 17, 1974, p. 13.

It is a search
Whose few invited searchers
Are often too close
To be objective

Friends tend to reflect
What one already knows and can see
Because friends, like oneself, tend
To be less objective and more receptive
To what has become familiar

Then looking for oneself
Becomes a task of finding a mirror
That reflects an image
That is not distorted

WAYS TO OVERCOME THE MYTH

1. Remember we are interdependent. Who I am is expressed through you and who you are comes through me. We cannot separate ourselves from others.

2. Create a list of five self-definitional and five self-evaluative beliefs. As you look at the finished list try to recall how you have arrived at these beliefs. Did your parents tell you? teachers? peers? Or, have you just "decided" on your own? If so, recall how people have reacted to you as you present yourself. Write a paper in which you discuss your thoughts, focusing upon how the beliefs developed and how people respond to you when you behave according to these beliefs.

3. Create a list of five self-definitional and five self-evaluative beliefs. From the list, create a collage using photographs, pictures from magazines and newspapers, even draw if necessary.

a. Ask a friend to make a collage of you, also. Compare the collages to see overlaps and differences. Discuss what you find. If similarities—what do you share that would permit both of you to see you in the same way? If differences—are they of degree or kind? That is, does the friend not include some of the beliefs you did because he doesn't know about them? or because he doesn't see them as important as some others?

b. Now you create a collage of another person and discuss the differences and similarities with him.

4. Create a list of 10 beliefs about yourself that you think are important (no one else will see them). Put the list away. Now, seek out a person in class who does not know you. Spend time getting to know each other.

a. Introduce the other person to the class and have the other introduce you. As you are introduced, look at your 10 important beliefs. Are they coming through in the words of the other? If not, then think about what you told him during your moments of talking together. Perhaps what beliefs are important to you, how you think of yourself, is not coming through in your conversations with other people. If you want people to respond to the real you, then you need to present the real you.

5. With another person practice the responses of confirmation, rejection and disconfirmation. It is important to know the difference between them in order to be able to monitor your behavior toward others.

a. Listen to a conversation between people you know who care for one another. Keep a record (in secret of course) of the number of remarks made which confirm, reject and/ or disconfirm the self-concept of one of them. What happens in the conversation when there is rejection or disconfirmation? How do the participants respond to one another once rejected or disconfirmed?

b. Listen carefully to your own conversations with people you care for. How often do you say things that reject or disconfirm the self-concept of the other? Ask the other how he feels when you do reject or disconfirm.

INSIGHT 5.5 "Please Hear What I'm Not Saying" by a 21-year-old patient at the Katherine Hamilton Mental Health Center, Terre Haute, Indiana.

Don't be fooled by me.
Don't be fooled by the face I wear,
For I wear a mask, a thousand masks,
  masks that I'm afraid to take off,
  and none of them are me.
Pretending is an art that's second nature with me,
  but don't be fooled, for God's sake, don't be fooled.
I give you the impression that I'm secure,
  that all is sunny and unruffled with me,
  within as well as without,
  that confidence is my name and coolness my game,
  that the water's calm, and I'm in command,
  and that I need no one.
But don't believe me.
Please.
My surface may seem smooth, but my surface is my mask,
  my ever-varying and ever-concealing mask.
Beneath lies no smugness, no complacence,
Beneath lies the real me in confusion, in fear, in aloneness.
But I hide this.
I don't want anybody to know it,
I panic at the thought of my weakness and fear being exposed.
That's why I frantically create a mask to hide behind,
  a nonchalant, sophisticated facade, to help me pretend,
  to shield me from the glance that knows.
But such a glance is precisely my salvation. My only salvation.
And I know it.
That is if it's followed by acceptance, if it's followed by love.
It's the only thing that can liberate me, from myself,
  from my own self-built prison walls,
  from the barriers that I so painstakingly erect.
It's the only thing that will assure me of what I can't
  assure myself,
  that I'm really worth something.
But I don't tell you this. I don't care to. I'm afraid to.
I'm afraid your glance won't be followed by acceptance and love.
I'm afraid you'll think less of me, that you'll laugh,
  and your laugh would kill me.
So I play my game, my desperate pretending game,
  with a facade of assurance without, and a trembling

child within.
And so begins the parade of masks,
        the glittering-by, empty parade of masks . . .
And my left becomes a front.
I idly chatter to you in the suave tones of surface talk.
I tell you everything that's really nothing,
        and nothing of what's everything, of what's crying
        within me.
So when I'm going through my routine do not be fooled by
        what I'm saying.
Please listen carefully and try to hear what I'm NOT saying,
        what I'd like to be able to say, what for survival I
        need to say,
        but what I can't say.
I dislike hiding. Honestly.
I dislike the superficial game I'm playing, the superficial,
        phony game.
I'd really like to be genuine and spontaneous, and me.
But you've got to help me.
You've got to hold out your hand
        even when that's the last thing I seem to want, or need.
Only you can call me to aliveness.
Only you can wipe away from my eyes the blank stare
        of the breathing dead.
Each time you're kind, and gentle, and encouraging,
        each time you try to understand because you really care,
        my heart begins to grow wings, very small wings, very
        feeble wings
        but wings.
With your sensitivity and sympathy, and your power of under-
        standing,
        you can breathe life into me. I want you to know that.
I want you to know how important you are to me, how you can be
        a creator of the person that is me if you choose to.
Please choose to.
You alone can break down the wall behind which I tremble.
You alone can release me from my shadow world of panic and
        uncertainty,
        from my lonely prison.
So do not pass me by.
It will not be easy for you.
A long conviction of worthlessness builds strong walls.
The nearer you approach me, the blinder I may strike back.
It's irrational, but despite what the books say about man,
        I am irrational.

I fight against the very thing that I cry out for. But I am
    told that love is stronger than strong walls, and in
    this lies my hope,
    my only hope.
Please try to beat down those walls with firm hands, but
    with gentle hands—for a child is very sensitive.
Who am I, you may wonder? I am someone you know very well.
For I am every man you meet and I am every woman you meet.

SUMMARY

A belief existing in our society asserts that each of us is independent of all others: who we are at any given time has nothing to do with people we make contact with. Our position has been that the belief is a myth: people are interdependent. How we see ourselves is a result of whom we contact and the types of interaction we experience together. In dispelling the myth, we noticed that the self-concept establishes a base-line of expectations for our behavior and of our expectations for the behavior of others toward us within any particular social setting. The self-concept is comprised of definitional statements and evaluative statements about ourselves. How we come to see ourselves grows from watching the behavior of others toward us in differing social settings. As we watch others respond to us, we can observe confirmation, rejection, or disconfirmation of the way in which we see ourselves.

In dispelling the myth, we present three generalizations which directly tie our relationship with others to our self-concept: (1) the greater the difference between our self-image and the image others have of us, the greater will be the chance for misunderstanding; (2) the greater the difference between how we see ourselves in the present and how we see our ideal selves, the greater will be the dissatisfaction with our communicative behaviors; (3) the greater the difference between the images others have of us and their ideal image of us, the less chance there is for a satisfactory relationship. Others' influence on us and our influence on others will be more fully illustrated as we discuss openness and self-disclosure in the following chapter.

6

OPENNESS AND SELF DISCLOSURE

MYTH
*"If You Can't Say Nothin' Nice,
Don't Say Nothin' At All."*

An advisee of mine was recently doing his student-teaching at a nearby high school. About half way through the experience, he stopped in my office and the following conversation took place.

Me: (lightly) "How are things going?"

He: (concerned and slightly frustrated) "I really don't know. Nobody, not the regular teacher or my supervisor, has ever said a word. They turn over the class and let me do my thing, but I've never once heard a comment about my performance. Oh, they say I'm doing 'fine' or 'that was nicely done' . . . . so I guess that means I'm doing all right. But I don't *feel* like I'm doing a very good job and I'm certainly *not learning* anything about how to run a classroom."

His superiors believed the myth. They assumed that he didn't want an honest and open appraisal of his performance, so they gave him short, quick, ritualized statements of approval. Instead, he wanted to know what his strengths and weaknesses were. He wanted some information about his teaching ability and not a passing, positive comment which told him nothing about how he was doing. Because he didn't get these honest criticisms, he

126

began to think that the supervisors were incompetent and incapable of guiding student-teachers. He was beginning to believe either that he was so good he intimidated them by comparison, or, that he was so bad he shouldn't become a teacher and their silence was the polite way of saying so. He didn't know what to believe about the supervisors or about his own abilities. Not getting any information, he became frustrated, confused and discouraged.

As individuals, we want to know how we are doing. We want to be appreciated and respected by those around us who we care for and work with. We know that not everything we do should be rewarded ("Nobody is perfect"), that some of our behaviors should be changed and can be improved. A professor blatantly stated this one day after class. He asked: "What am I doing wrong? Things just don't seem to be going right." One student replied, "Everything is fine. You are a good teacher. Don't degrade yourself." He angrily retorted, "I know I'm a good teacher, but I want to be better. Don't patronize me, I don't wanna hear it. I'm better than that and so are you." He wanted an honest perception of how he was doing. Not getting it, he was slowly losing confidence in himself and respect for those he was trying to educate. The giving of straightforward, honest perceptions requires that we trust each other enough to be open.

THE NEED FOR OPENNESS

As we've stated many times, communication occurs when two persons realize that they have shared referential and relational meanings. This does not necessarily imply that the persons have agreed on *a* meaning for some event, but only claims they have realized each is being understood. In other words, communication is sharing. But a sharing of what? It is a sharing of ourselves with another; allowing another to experience some part of the world as we see it; allowing ourselves to experience some part of the world as they see it. When we have communicated, we have shared with another those qualities, meanings, ideas, and feelings of our own that make each of us a unique

127

individual. Actually, we cannot become unique individuals unless we share parts of ourselves with others. In order for us to know what kind of individuals we are, we must compare ourselves with at least one other on some topic. By comparing ourselves with another, we can determine our similarities and differences. Awareness of these differences makes us aware of our individuality.

To understand one's self and be conscious of one's individuality one needs to be understood by at least one other person. But, to be understood by another person, one also needs to understand the other, to be cognizant of the feelings, ideas and qualities which make the other a unique individual. Some ideas and feelings the two of us will hold in common; others will be different and sometimes in conflict. Either way, if we each know where the other stands, then we have shared parts of ourselves with each other and we can both find our individuality. In other words, our own individuality is made known to us and others only in the context of an interpersonal relationship. There is no other way. A person who isolates himself from others and claims to be his own man, who asserts his individuality in isolation, asserts no individuality. He denies his right to be an individual. If I am to know myself, I must be known to others.

> It is only through . . . sharing that a person comes to *know himself*. Introspection of itself is helpless. A person can confide all of his secrets to the docile pages of his personal diary, but he can know himself and experience the fullness of life only in the meeting with another person. Friendship becomes a great adventure (Powell, 1969, p. 98).

A familiar example may help to show this reciprocal pattern between knowing oneself, knowing others and being known by others. A female college student came to see me one day. She was about to graduate from college with a degree in elementary education. (Her father had assured her that that would be a "good profession" for her and that she "could always get a job.") She was worried, moderately depressed and felt guilty about feeling depressed. Her parents had provided a good life, plenty of clothes, food and spending money. She had taken piano lessons ("Everyone should have an appreciation of music," her mother had told her) and had worked while in college

("Working builds character," her father had assured her). She was planning on getting married after summer graduation to a fellow who had a good job and would make a good husband and father ("At least, that's what everyone said"). She would start teaching in the fall at a good school. Although she didn't really like her student teaching ("The students scared me to death."), she assured me that she'd be happy teaching third-grade. But, she said, "Something is lacking, there doesn't seem to be any meaning to my life. Where am I going? I must really be screwed up in the head to not feel great about what's happening to me." My question to her was: "What do you want? What really turns you on? Don't tell me what you should do or enjoy, but ask yourself what do you really like?" She looked at me, confused, and hesitatingly said: "No one ever asked me what *I* wanted before. I don't even know if I've ever asked myself that question. I always thought I knew what to do, and had made up my own mind, but . . . I wonder, did I decide? Or, because I had an opinion, did I think I'd decided? But," she continued with increased concern, "if those things I say I want are not what I want, who am I?"

INSIGHT 6.1   Who Am I?

Today, many of us are asking: "Who am I?" It has come to be a socially fashionable question. The implication is that I do not really know my own self as a person. We have said that my person is what I think, judge, feel, etc. If I have communicated these things freely and openly, as clearly as I can and as honestly as I can, I will find a noticeable growth in my own sense of identity as well as a deeper and more authentic knowledge of the other. It has come to be a psychological truism that *I will understand only as much of myself as I have been willing to communicate to another.*

(Powell, 1969, p. 80, emphasis my own)

If we are to share parts of our experience, we must be open and honest with others and with ourselves. Through open and honest disclosures, spontaneously given in the context of a trusting relationship, we can share ourselves with another. In so doing, we learn about ourselves and others. But what does it mean to be open? What does one do and say in order to be genuinely open with another?

MEANING OF OPENNESS

Openness often refers to the reception of a wide range of divergent information from a variety of sources. In this sense, openness is characterized by a willingness to listen to opinions, information, and perceptions that are discrepant with one's own. When people remind us to "be more open-minded," they mean that we should "listen to what the other guy has to say."

But, we consider openness to be a characteristic of verbal messages, not a personal quality. Openness refers to types of verbal statements which contain certain kinds of information. People who frequently transmit open statements are generally called "open" and "straightforward." Hopefully, people who transmit open messages will become more healthy and authentic (Jourard, 1968, 1971) and better able to adapt and grow. But, the concept of openness refers to a characteristic of verbal messages and not to types of people.

The basic characteristic of open messages is the degree of personalization involved (MacDoniels et al., 1971), the degree to which the speaker verbally transmits information about himself which the listener is unlikely to know or discover. An open statement carries with it the relational implication that the speaker is willing to be known, to share some personal experience with the listener. From the listener's point-of-view, open statements imply that the speaker is honestly trying to share himself and invite the listener to reciprocate. The importance of open verbal behavior in establishing understanding and a communication-state is that these expressions more readily allow the two persons to mutually define their relationship. By more clearly specifying where each person stands on a particular issue, both persons can more accurately define where they stand on a certain issue. Do they agree or disagree? If they agree, what can they both do together to resolve the problem, if a problem is being discussed. (Realizing that you agree is not as easy as it sounds. For instance, how often have you had a heated argument with another only to discover that you were both saying the same thing?) If persons disagree, on what do they differ? If each person concentrates on objectively stating his own position rather than evaluating the other's, then the probability of resolving the difference increases. Of course, one resolution to any difference of opinion is to respect the other's opinions and refuse to let the difference affect the relationship.

For instance, a good friend of mine is an avid hunter. He thoroughly enjoys stalking through the woods, tracking and tailing the deer until the kill. He always eats what he kills (going as long as five months without buying meat from the grocery store), which is quite a savings. He respects nature and is never intentionally cruel or careless to the wildlife or the environment. His hunting equipment is meticulously cared for and not handled foolishly or dangerously. Dick seems to honestly enjoy hunting (his thrill and pride in getting an 8-point buck is unmistakable), and does it well. However, I personally can't do it. I like to watch the animals, to be surrounded by the peace and beauty of the woods, and frequently camp and back-pack. But I just can't cope with the thought of killing a deer or rabbit.

Nonetheless this difference of opinion has not affected our growing friendship. We frequently are handball partners, play on the same softball team, help each other with yard work, and get together for drinks and social evenings. We have agreed to disagree on this issue and don't let this disagreement affect the respect and acceptance we have for each other. We do not let it interfere with our sharing of other experiences and ourselves.

INSIGHT 6.2   From *Notes to Myself* by Hugh Prather*

No one is wrong. At most someone is uninformed. If I think a man is wrong, either I am unaware of something, or he is. So unless I want to play a superiority game I had best find out what he is looking at.

"You're wrong" means "I don't understand you"—I'm not seeing what you're seeing. But there is nothing *wrong* with you, you are simply not me and that's not wrong.

*Hugh Prather, *Notes to Myself* (Moab, Utah: Real People Press, 1970).

Borrowing heavily from MacDoniels et al.,(1971),* an *open expression* is defined as one which reveals thoughts, intentions, feelings, and perceptions about some aspects of the environment (self, others, events, behaviors) that is directly related to the immediate situation. An open expression, then, states the speaker's personal perception (*whose*) of something or someone in his environment (*what*) that is important in the "here and now" (*when*) which includes some behavioral evidence or reason for his perception (*why*).

CRITERIA FOR MESSAGE OPENNESS

When trying to understand any message, the listener should ask himself four basic questions: (1) *Whose* opinion, belief, feeling is being expressed? (2) *What* specific event, perception, feeling, belief, value, etc. is being expressed? (3) *When,* in what situation, is the opinion transmitted claimed to be relevant? and (4) *Why,* what is the basis of the opinion believed or the feeling that occurred? The more precisely the listener can answer these questions, the more open the transmitted message.

Whose: The Speaker's Own Personal Point Of View

This characteristic is the most basic dimension of openness and refers to the degree of "I-ness" contained within the verbal message. The more the individual takes clear responsibility for the perception expressed, the more open the message. There is no doubt about whose opinion is being transmitted; it's the speaker's. The more the speaker asserts that the thought transmitted belongs to some vague collection of people, the harder

---

*These authors at the Communication Research Center at the University of Kansas also believe that openness refers to message transmission and not reception, but they assert that it is a relational characteristic which differentiates interpersonal relationships. We, however, disagree. It is our contention that openness is a message variable, and that the relational dimension of concern would be the amount of trust existing in the interpersonal relationship. The frequency with which open statements are transmitted between two or more persons should be an indication of the level of trust and the growth potential existing in their relationship.

for the listener to know the speaker's stance on the perceptions expressed and the less open the message. This criterion for judging the openness of messages forms a continuum from "I" to some unidentifiable "Other." The continuum can be broken into five discrete categories: (a) "I." The speaker clearly takes responsibility for the perception; (b) "We." The speaker includes himself in a group which shares ownership of the information presented; (c) "Some of us." The speaker implies some identifiable group, but the listener is unsure whether the speaker includes himself in that group; (d) "The American Public." The speaker specifically names some large collection of people whose idea is being expressed but which belief is practically unknowable and not easily verified; and (e) "Some people." The speaker vaguely refers to some collection of individuals who "have" the perception transmitted. There is no way of verifying that the people would assert the belief since the speaker identifies no specific group.

In the first two categories, the speaker specifically informs the listener he believes or owns the perception expressed, either alone ("I") or with others ("We"). The listener is explicitly informed where the other person stands on the issue. He can readily evaluate where he and the speaker stand in relationship to each other. In the remaining three categories the judgment of where the speaker and listener stand in relation to each other becomes increasingly inferential and less accurate. The more inferences one has to make in order to understand the other's meaning, the more one reads in his own biases, interpretations, meanings, feelings, and the less accurate his understanding of the speaker's intended meaning.

For instance, "Some students are distracted and offended by your pipe smoking, Dr. Millar" is a statement I recently received. Is this particular student distracted and offended? Is the student being diplomatic and kind towards the person who gives out grades or was she just reporting what other students have said? In other words, how does this particular student feel about my pipe smoking? One can only guess. But the more one has to guess and infer where the speaker stands on the opinion expressed, the greater the likelihood that misunderstandings and distortions will occur between those two persons.

When generalized collections of people are stated to own the feeling or perception, very little information is provided about the collective. For instance, "The American people believe that vasectomies take the worry out of being close" is a statement that supposedly asserts something about Americans. But, who are "The American People"? How does the speaker know that vasectomies and not deodorants take the worry out of being close? Does the speaker actually believe that all Americans feel this way? Does the speaker actually expect the listener to accept this statement as a valid characteristic of some collective called Americans? If more than 50% of Americans do believe, which ones? city-dwellers, farmers, Blacks, Chicanos, Whites, Northerners, housewives, executives? How does the speaker know they believe this . . . has he taken a poll? Has he read a poll? Or, does the speaker generalize from the three persons he just talked to? The point is when generalized sources are stated to believe or feel something, the listener cannot assess the information in the message, nor can he understand the speaker's stance on the particular belief asserted. Therefore, he cannot readily determine where he stands in relationship to the speaker —communication becomes difficult, if not impossible.

As Bertrand Russell has said, "Subjective certainty is inversely proportional to objective certainty." This means that the larger the number of people claimed to hold the belief of the speaker, the more unwilling the speaker is to state his own personal feelings and opinions. The more the speaker hides behind collections of others, the less responsibility he assumes for the information presented, the more difficult becomes the task of understanding the speaker, and the less likely interpersonal contact is between the speaker and listener.

What: The Origin Of The Information Is Clearly Specified

This dimension refers to the origin of the speaker's perception, feeling, or thought. If other people are referred to, then this dimension can be broken into the same categories as the "ownership" dimension. In this case the categories would be: (a) a particular person is explicitly referred to ("John, you make me mad."); (b) an identifiable group is specified and the other person is clearly included in that group ("Mary, your work group is not very efficient."); (c) an identifiable group is specified but the other person is not directly included in the group ("You know, Bob, some people in our department are lazy."); (d) a large collective is named but the collective's position is essentially unknowable ("College students are trying to destroy my way of life." or "The military-industrial complex is trying to get us." or "Anyone over thirty can't be trusted."); (e) a vague, unidentifiable collection of people are claimed to be the source of the perception or feeling ("Some people make me angry." or "Many people are ripping me off.").

The principle of specificity also applies when events are stated to be the origins of one's perceptions. The more specific the message in pin-pointing what events or what aspects of the events are being discussed, the more easily the listener can understand the speaker. For instance, our parents thoroughly enjoy going to hockey games and are avid fans. Our father and mother could both say "Hockey games are very exciting." This statement is an evaluative conclusion and is similar in specificity to the above category 'd' (i.e., a large identifiable collective). But our father's enjoyment of the game is primarily based on the speed, finesse and action of the players. To make a more open statement, he might say: "Hockey games are very exciting and I like going to them. The players must be agile and coordinated for the game moves at a fast pace. Players may skate as fast as 30 miles per hour and the puck often travels around 100 miles per hour. I think watching a right-winger skate toward the goal on a break-away is one of the most exciting events in sports."

Our mother's enjoyment of hockey, however, stems as much from watching the crowd and dynamics between the players and the spectators as it does from the activities on the ice. Her open expression of this enjoyment might go something like this: "Attending a hockey game is really quite a thrilling experience for me. The fans are rabid and boisterously announce their approval or disapproval of happenings on the ice. There is always an electricity in the air which I've never sensed at other sporting events. One can almost feel the ebb and flow of energy and excitement that moves from spectator to players, from players to spectators and back again. No question about it, I am an avid hockey fan."

Neither of these interpretations are more right or better than the other, they are simply different and an open message explicitly deals with the difference. In summary, when what is referred to is made explicit, the message is more open; the more likely the listener is to understand the speaker; and the more likely the speaker and listener are to share meanings.

When: Open Messages Address The Immediate Situation

This characterisitc of open messages refers to the statement's space-time relevance. Does the message concern our activities right here and right now? Is it related to something already done or something that might happen? Or, is no indication given as to when and where the information asserted is relevant? This characteristic of open messages can be thought of as a continuum and broken into four categories for examination. The first two categories contain messages that relate to the immediate situation while the last two categories are those which are not directly relevant to the present interaction. The categories are: (a) here and now, (b) there and now, (c) there and not now, (d) no spatial-temporal reference given. The more open the expression, the more it relates to the "here and now." For instance, "At the moment, I feel very close to you" is an expression tied to the immediate situation (here and now). The comment does not necessarily imply the speaker had previously felt close to the other or that he/she will continue to feel close. But at this point in time, he/she does feel close to the other person.

A "there and now" statement would contain a reference to a perception that had previously occurred but has relevance to the present. "I am still mad at you for what you did at Mother's." Or, "Some of us disagree with the policy you've been advocating and are here to discuss it." Both messages refer to previous events but have clues relating to the speaker's present feelings and intentions.

"There and then" expressions recount previous perceptions which are not part of one's immediate feelings or intentions; as when someone laughingly states "Man, was I mad at you when

136

you spilled the beer at the party." Or, "Some people used to think you were cold and conceited." Both of these messages assert previous perceptions. Neither tells what the speaker does feel now, only that his perception differs from what it was. To be told that others used to perceive you as "cold and conceited" implies they don't anymore, but it does not inform the listener of current perceptions. The omission of present perceptions and feelings does not help the listener evaluate his current condition and relationship with the speaker.

"There and not now" statements tell the listener that what was, no longer is. The message information is incomplete in terms of helping the interactors mutually define their current interpersonal relationship. A great deal of our typical conversation patterns fall into this category. Telling stories, recounting past events, and talking about old acquaintances are things we frequently do and enjoy. These activities can make the present situation fun, light and non-threatening, and so they have some social usefulness in human interactions. People can't always explore each other's uniqueness. We haven't the time or energy to understand and share meaning with everyone we meet. So, we must sometimes engage in light, entertaining conversations. But, however useful and entertaining these "there and then" expressions might be, they are not directly relevant to the present situation, and do not necessarily help the parties involved understand each other. "There and not now" statements are not open.

Statements that don't include space and time references are hard to interpret since they have no necessary relevance to the immediate situations. For instance, a girl says to her date, "I sure do like almond-mint chocolate ice-cream." "Shall we go get some?" "No thanks." Or, "Sometimes people really upset me." (Is this one of the times?) Or "Every now and then I like to do something crazy." (Tonight?) The listener can't tell if the message suggests action, or if it is just said for social reasons. A statement like this appears to have no relevance to us or our present transaction. In terms of the information contained within the verbalized message, the listener has no way of knowing when the perception, feeling, or thought expressed is operative.

Frequent transmission of these kinds of statements that

have no space-time relevance can lead to the dangerous confusion of facts and evaluations. If one says often enough "The President is not doing his job," he can come to believe that this is a factual statement about the President, rather than his own personal evaluation. Perhaps the President is not doing a satisfactory job, but this statement doesn't carry a specific message. Nothing is known about the President's performance from the above statement. All that can be inferred is that the speaker doesn't like the President. Confusion of personal evaluations with verifiable facts breeds misunderstanding.

Why: Open Messages Cite Behavioral Evidence For The Information Expressed

The behavioral evidence dimension of open messages refers to why the speaker feels, thinks, or intends what he does. This aspect of openness is concerned with the behaviors on which the speaker bases the information he transmits. The more behaviorally specific the justification given for the perception expressed, the more open the message. The rationale for including this aspect in openness is that when the speaker explicitly states why and on what behaviors his perceptions are based, the listener can understand his message more readily and the more likely they are to communicate. In other words, the degree of behavioral specificity is the underlying aspect of this dimension which provides the reason, rationale, or cause for one's perception.

This behavioral dimension of openness can be broken into the following categories for examination: (a) a specific behavior is cited as the reason for the information expressed ("Karen, you make me feel worthwhile when you do little things for me, like fixing me a martini, holding my hand at parties or playing my favorite records on the stereo."); (b) a class or set of behaviors is explicitly referred to but no specific behavior is mentioned ("Karen, you make me feel worthwhile when you do little things you know I like." or "You make me angry when you are inconsiderate."); (c) a class or set of behaviors is implied but the type of behaviors alluded to are not stated in the message ("Some of the things you do really turn me on." or "Sometimes you seem to go out of your way to make me upset.");

(d) no behavioral reasons are stated or implied, no justification is given for the information expressed ("Karen, you make me mad." or "Wow, does she turn me on.").

As we progress from specifically mentioned behaviors to no reasons cited, we move from thoughtful decisions to judgments. Decisions can be discussed and negotiated in a relatively non-threatening manner. Judgments, however, tend to be evaluative in nature, encouraging defensive responses which increase the use of threats. Threats decrease the likelihood of trust and understanding (Deutsch & Krauss, 1962). Consequently, their use decreases the likelihood of reaching a communication-state.

Decisions are more tentative than judgments since they specify a probable relationship between some set of behaviors and some assertion. Judgments state an absolute property of something or person. When a decision is made, the possibility of reaching a new and different decision remains if new evidence is produced. Decisions, then, are consciously made and are similar to scientific hypotheses. Judgments, on the other hand, assert some belief which is assumed to be true. A judgment includes the implication that evidence is provided.

The distinction between judgments and decisions is a subtle one: judgment expresses a belief, perception, or evaluation which is claimed to be absolutely true and which implies the speaker will not change his mind. If pushed, the speaker may find reasons, behaviors and/or statistics which support his view. The speaker's mind is set before he looks for supporting evidence. A decision, on the other hand, states that, given a set of reasons, behaviors, and/or statistics the speaker has decided to accept a certain perception as the most accurate one. A different decision may be possible. There is more than one way of appraising the situation, but this is where the speaker stands at the moment. Negotiation and mutual understanding are possible, because the reasons for the belief are specified with the implication that different reasons may lead to a different decision.

To summarize, the more behaviorally specific the information presented, the more open the message; the more likely it is for two persons to come to understand *what* each is saying and *why;* and the more likely it is they will reach a state of communication.

INSIGHT 6.3　　　Summary of Openness Criteria

OPEN— — — — — — — — — — — — — — — — — NOT OPEN

Whose:	I	We	Some of us	Americans	Everybody
What:					
(Person)	John	Your group, Esther	Some of you	People who	Others
(Object)	This can opener	Electric can openers	Household appliances	Mechanical things	Everything
When:	Right now	I'm still upset	Was I proud	I have been depressed	I love dandelions
Why:	Slapping	Your aggres- siveness	Some things you do	Those things	Everything you do

SELF-DISCLOSURE

An important subset of openness is verbalizations which reveal the feelings and emotions an individual is experiencing now. The expression of emotional reactions being felt in the here-now defines self-disclosure. We conceive of self-disclosure as the expression of personal feelings that one has about himself, about the social situation and about the people in it at the time the feelings are experienced. If we are to understand others, then we must understand our own feelings. Yet, for us to understand our feelings, we've got to express them.

If I rely on others to infer my feelings from my behavior, then I leave their understanding of my emotions and behavior subject to their interpretation—I must hope their interpretations match mine. To ensure better accuracy, then, I need to tell others how I feel at the time I feel it. Jourard (1971), who has probably researched and written most about self-disclosure, makes the connection between disclosing the self and the development of self-concept, when he states as fact, "No man can come to know himself except as an outcome of disclosing himself to another person" ((Jourard, 1971, p. 6).

Openness And Disclosure Aid Understanding

Openness and self-disclosure with others work together to help them understand us and us, them. The best source of information about you is you. If you self-disclose, then I can see your uniqueness as an individual, your emotions. If you are open, then I am able to better interpret your disclosure of feelings, attitudes, and beliefs to me.

There is a teacher in the Physical Education department of our university who is considered a "real bastard" when it comes to permitting students to miss class. He is considered a "bastard" by students because of the way in which he laughs and makes cynical cracks about reasons they have for missing class or assignments. One day after a noon game of basketball with him, I asked him about his reputation. He took me to his office where he showed me a dittoed sheet of 74 of the most used student excuses for missing classes. He pointed out that he'd been teaching for nearly 25 years, and that there weren't too many new reasons students could give for cutting class. Furthermore, he pointed out that he had been conned a number of times and so had been the butt of a number of jokes about gullible professors. His cynicism about student excuses for missing class and not doing the work assigned, then, is based upon nearly a quarter of a century of experience. If the students he now has could understand "where he was coming from" I don't think they would feel so strongly about his being a "bastard." Don't get me wrong. I'm not condoning his insensitivity to real reasons for missing class. What I am saying is that factual information which comes from the past may be very relevant to observers in the present as they try to interpret the behavior of this particular teacher. If he was open about his experiences with students' excuses over the past 25 years, and disclosed his feeling when students gave excuses, his present students would be in a much better position to understand his feelings. Certainly, they would be in a better position to under-

141

stand his intensity of feeling. (Notice, too, that students shaped his self-concept and behavior by making fun of him, by rejection of the faculty person he tried to be as a young teacher.)

Let me give you another example of how openness and self-disclosure work together. A neighbor of ours is terrified of our dog, a German shepherd. We consider him a gentle "lover dog," but our neighbor considers Rusty a frightening, potentially dangerous animal. Recently, this friend was out jogging in the early morning hours and caught Rusty unaware. The dog jumped up, charged to the edge of our property, barking authoritatively. Our friend was absolutely petrified. He expressed his fear of Rusty to me (self-disclosure) when, on hearing the dog barking, I went out to see what was going on and put Rusty on a leash. But, I wasn't able to understand the intensity of the fear until his wife told me later that he has been bitten by a number of dogs on different occasions during his years as a police officer. He has seen torn bodies of children who were attacked by dogs running wild. The point is that for me to fully understand the disclosure about his here/now feeling of fear, I needed factual information about his there/then experiences to provide a framework within which I could interpret his feeling.

Disclosure And Self-Concept

The here/now disclosure of attitudes, values, feelings and beliefs held by the self is most likely to encourage growth and development of you as an individual. Why? Because attitudes, values, feelings and beliefs are what make us different from other individuals, and hence, unique. As we begin to verbalize these, to reveal them to ourselves and to others, we are in a better position to understand what constitutes our basic line of behavior. Once you have disclosed these attitudes and beliefs, others are in a better position to respond directly to them—to confirm, to reject, or to disconfirm them. So, you grow in the sense that another area of you is responded to, and your relationships grow in the sense that another is better able to understand your behavior.

This process of disclosing and responding and the consequent growth in self-concept has been graphically depicted by the Johari Window (Luft, 1970). Created by Luft and Ingham, the conceptualization assumes the presence of behaviors, attitudes, and motivations which are known and unknown to ourselves and to others. They visualize the information in a window-like model:

	Known to Self	Not Known to Self
Known to Others	OPEN	BLIND
Not Known to Others	HIDDEN	UNKNOWN

The OPEN quadrant reflects the behaviors, attitudes, and motivations that are known to both the self and the people around you. The BLIND quadrant represents those areas of behavior, attitude, and motivation hidden to us but seen by others. The Scope mouthwash commercials on TV exemplify a part of ourselves (bad breath?) that others may see but to which we are blind. The HIDDEN quadrant represents aspects of ourselves that we know but do not wish to disclose to others (for whatever reason!). The UNKNOWN quadrant represents those areas of self that neither you nor I are aware of—the hidden motivations that seem to drive us in ways that we can't explain.

The objective of self-disclosure is to change the configuration of the window to enlarge the Open quadrant while decreasing the Hidden and Blind quadrants. The Unknown quadrant would decrease in area also, but not as much as the other two. When self-disclosure between two people has occurred over time, the Johari Window will look like the following for a single individual:

	Known to Self	Not Known to Self
Known to Others	OPEN	BLIND
Not Known to Others	HIDDEN	UNKNOWN

143

If we each disclose to the other, then we know more about the other, are better able to predict (and hence, understand) the behavior of the other and have a better knowledge of our separate selves, since more has been exposed and responded to. Again, the conclusion is that my growth as a human being and the conception I have of myself is affected by what I show you and how you respond to me.

If two persons are constantly trying to say something "nice," then over time the topics of conversation become severely limited. Why? Because agreement, not understanding, becomes the prime criterion for talk. The principal concern for choosing content becomes not-making-the-other-upset. No two individuals can ever have exactly the same feelings, perceptions and connotations. If these inevitable differences—however minimal—are not discussed and explored, if conversations are geared to being "nice" and not open, then the individuality of each person is denied and/or avoided. The two, as individuals, cannot share, grow and communicate because neither transmits the uniqueness of self.

The other day when I was talking about self-disclosure in class, an ex-Air Force sergeant raised his hand and said, "There are some situations in which self-disclosure won't work. It's not appropriate to tell my commanding officer how I feel about him, either now or five years from now, so long as he remains my commanding officer." That was a useful statement for him to make, because it forced the class to think about a crucial issue in self-disclosure—not whether one should disclose or what one should disclose, but when one should disclose to another person. Let's look at when disclosure is appropriate.

CRITERIA FOR DISCLOSURE

The making of open statements is both time-consuming and risky. We often don't have or can't take the time to state the basis for our beliefs. As a general rule, don't make open comments unless you are willing to invest both the time and energy necessary to make sure that you are being understood. In other words, don't make statements that encourage discussion and negotiation unless you are willing to discuss and negotiate. Being willing to negotiate implies a willingness to change one's point of view, the courage to be imperfect, and the willingness to accept one's mistakes without unduly blaming oneself or the other for pointing them out.

Disclosure of much of the information about the self is a matter of choice. We know best, if imperfectly, what we believe and feel. We can conceal those beliefs and feelings from others if we wish to expend the energy to conceal them. (It's a little more difficult nonverbally, but it is possible, and all of us have practiced such deception.) What we disclose, then, is a matter of choice. When to disclose is also a matter of choice. In deciding appropriateness, we need to decide first if the existing relationship is between persons or roles.

Person-To-Person Relationship

Our argument is that openness and disclosure of self are important when you are attempting to establish, maintain, or change a person-to-person relationship. For example, a married man and woman passing through their years of deepening love; two neighbor children becoming bosom friends throughout their lifetimes; newly-acquired college roommates "getting into" one another—all need to disclose if they are to continue to grow and develop. If the relationship between them is role-to-role (i.e., teacher-to-student, employer-to-employee, colleague-to-colleague), then the notion of disclosing self becomes almost irrelevant. We say "almost," because even in a role-to-role situation, some disclosure of self may help another better interpret the actions and behaviors he sees you perform in your role. Role-to-role disclosure is "irrelevant" to the extent that how you feel as an individual today on the assembly line at Ford in Detroit has nothing to do with how the foreman relates to you as a worker. The relationship between foreman and worker is not going to change through your disclosures; therefore, disclosure is irrelevant. Because it is irrelevant, it is also inappropriate.

Disclosure of feelings in role situations may even be detrimental. "Whaddya trying' to do? Butter up the boss with that

145

'I like workin' for you' stuff?" Or, the information may be used against you in the competitive politics of the organization. In a study, Slobin, Miller, and Porter (Cozby, 1973) found that the greatest amount of disclosure was between fellow workers with the same status within a business organization. However, there was more disclosure to immediate supervisors than to immediate subordinates. Cozby hypothesizes that the disclosure to superiors may be an ingratiating technique to gain favor. The reason that people are reluctant to disclose to subordinates may be partially explained by the "reverse halo effect" discussed by Egan (1970, p. 211). The reverse halo effect is based upon an incorrect assumption that self-disclosure means revealing the worst of one's self. In an organizational setting, given this mistaken assumption, a supervisor would be reluctant to disclose for fear that his error or incompetence in one area (i.e., family problems) might be generalized by his subordinates to behavior in other areas. Certainly, such a generalization could be severely detrimental to a relationship. The first criterion for disclosure, then, deals with the kind of relationship, whether person-to-person or role-to-role.

Expectation Of A Deep Relationship

The second major criterion has to do with the quality of the relationship—the importance of, or the expectation of, a deepening relationship between two people. When we meet a person for the first time, or re-meet someone we've known earlier, there is usually time spent in chit-chat—a vying for position and gaining information about the other person. If the chit-chat has been pleasant and mutually rewarding to the individuals involved, then they may wish to deepen the relationship. So, they risk rejection by the other and disclose thoughts, feelings, attitudes, and facts about themselves, permitting the other to know them more fully. They run the risk, expecting that the resulting relationship will be deeper and more rewarding than the present one.

Our expectations for relationships and the kinds of behavior we look for in others are largely determined by our past experiences. We look for familiar kinds of behavior—kinds that we have heard and seen in the past. If a person makes statements

146

that have been made in the past by others whom you found trustworthy enough to risk disclosure with, and if he behaves in the manner of others to whom you have disclosed before, then you are likely to take the risk of disclosure. The expectation of a deepening relationship provides the second criterion for disclosing self to others.

REASONS WE AVOID OPENNESS AND DISCLOSURE

If openness and disclosure of self are so important to the establishment, maintenance, and change of relationships between people, why are we seemingly reluctant to disclose ourselves to others? Let's turn our attention to a few explanations.

Sociological Reasons

Sociological reasons given to explain why self-disclosure does not readily occur in the United States are: (a) disclosure signifies weakness, and (b) a society-wide cultivation of the lie is a way of life.

Self-disclosure signifies weakness. Egan (1970) says that we tend to reward the individual who suffers in silence. The idea of confession, of making the self known to others, is seen as weakness in our culture. He points out that such weakness might be understandable and even excused and encouraged in a woman. Cozby (1973), from his examination of self-disclosure literature, draws the conclusion that there was less self-disclosure by men than by women. He concludes that the lack of male disclosure may indicate a real difference between the sexes in terms of the willingness to express intimacies about one's self. Certainly, if the male role is expected to be strong in our culture, and if disclosing one's self is a sign of weakness, then we would be less likely to find men disclosing themselves. If self-disclosure isn't seen as a weakness, it is at least considered exhibitionistic (Egan, 1970). Our society apparently considers it improper to talk about one's self in a self-revealing manner, particularly for men.

The other cultural reason which Egan offers is that lying is seen as an integral part of Western society. Egan is not referring to the observation that we all lie once in awhile, but that the American culture, in fact, rewards and encourages lying. If a lie will protect, if a lie will bring gain, then the end justifies the means. The rewarding of lies discourages honest explorations of feelings and inhibits our willingness and ability to self-disclose.

Psychological Reasons

The four psychological reasons Egan offers are: (a) people fear knowing about themselves, (b) people fear intimacy, (c) people fear taking responsibility for another individual, and (d) the reverse halo effect. The fourth reason, the reverse halo effect, has already been described as the belief that disclosure reveals the "worst" of one's self. Let's briefly explain the first three.

First of all, people fear getting in touch with themselves. They fear that if they fully disclose and understand themselves, then somehow they will discover themselves to be less than they wish—and being less is intolerable. As a result, they avoid disclosing, and so avoid truly getting in touch with themselves.

The second psychological reason people avoid disclosure is that some people just plain fear intimacy. They are not afraid to get in touch with themselves, but they do fear letting others get in touch with them. They don't want contact with others. They fear the establishment of human relationships based upon emotional awareness, which may lead to intimacy.

The third reason is a flight from responsibility. Here, Egan suggests that to disclose one's self to another implies a willingness to change. Change requires effort and responsibility for one's actions. Therefore, avoiding public disclosure avoids assuming responsibility for undergoing personal change in attitudes, beliefs, values, and behaviors.

Perhaps these four psychological barriers to self-disclosure found within the individual may be generalized into the statement from John Powell's *Why Am I Afraid To Tell You Who I Am?:*

"I'm afraid to tell you who I am, because, if I tell you who I am, you might not like who I am, and it's all that I have."
(1967, p. 12)

148

In other words, I am who I am. If you cannot like, tolerate, forgive, and love who I am, then your reaction undercuts my very being. Rather than risk the cut, I avoid telling you who I am. But, in failing to disclose to you, I also fail to expose myself for your confirmation, or rejection, and so withhold from myself areas of myself. Those areas may need change, may be beautiful, or may bring to other people great pleasure and strength.

These individual fears and cultural pressures breed a resistance to permitting others to know you, a resistance to change. Wallace writes (Jessor and Feshbach, 1967), the resistance to change identity may be so strong, people will sacrifice life rather than change. Stories of people who kill themselves rather than face public disclosure fill our mass entertainment media.

Less dramatic ways for avoiding disclosure have been identified and categorized by contemporary authors. Some write about them as games, some as ego-defenses, some as defense mechanisms, some as defensive climates. The point is that people use a number of techniques to avoid disclosure by increasing the "psychological" distance between themselves and others. Winthrop, in his article on blocked communication and modern alienation, asserts that relationship difficulties between people spring "not from failures in and breakdowns of communication, but rather from the deliberate attempt to avoid communication" (1963, p. 98). From our perspective, alienation springs from the intent to avoid sharing ourselves with others and witnessing their reactions to us.

Realizing that we run the risk of trying to list and categorize an infinite number of different behavioral patterns which avoid communication, and knowing that it's not possible here to make such a cataloguing, the few that we will describe provide only a representative sample.

METHODS USED TO AVOID SELF-DISCLOSURE

One method for avoiding disclosure is to convert a potential communication situation into a one-way message flow. One person does all the talking and all the directing, and does not permit the other person to actively participate. We've often witnessed this characteristic in new teachers in the classroom for the first time. In their desire to avoid embarrassment, to retain control of the classroom, they make teaching a one-way sending of messages. The students are not allowed to react or interact or give feedback. There is no opportunity for a sharing of the control of the situation. Rather, all opportunity for communication is squelched, because all the messages are traveling in one direction.

Another method of avoiding self-revealment is to simply cut off the interaction. Physically leaving the scene is one way of cutting off the interaction so as to avoid disclosure. Another way is to carefully change the topic of conversation. Let's eavesdrop on a conversation which has been taking place between friends for several minutes:

"I just can't get into sex. It isn't that I never found anybody who's willing. It's just that I don't want to go to bed with anybody. I want intercourse to be an expression of a deep relationship; one that is important to me."

"Oh, you're just saying that. Everybody wants to have a good time once in awhile. You're no different. Why don't you admit it to yourself?"

"No, I really feel that way. And I'm beginning to think that some of your callous attitude about sexual relations is strictly a cover-up of your own feelings. I'm beginning to think that you hoped that sex would be meaningful, too, and you haven't found it to be."

"That makes me think of a book I just read. The central character is this guy who . . ."

The third method of avoiding disclosure and one that is more prevalent among the adults in our society than it is among people under 25, is to insist upon "polite" conversation. Remember the old adage, "Never discuss religion or politics"? Why? They're essentially both emotionally based, that's why. Somehow, attitudes, values, and feelings are supposed to be inappropriate conversation topics in "polite" company. During one of my first teacher workshops on interpersonal communication, the facilitator said we would be talking about feelings. To that, one of the older teachers in the group responded, "Only klutzes talk about emotions in public!" That was a comment guaranteed to put a damper on the group atmosphere! She might have been fearful about the whole prospect of discussing her feelings, and therefore, rejected the exercise as being in bad taste.

A fourth method for avoiding self-disclosure is to make the other person feel "one down" in the relationship. Through particular verbal and nonverbal message patterns, we can tell the other of his inadequacy or unimportance in our eyes. "One down" has super-negative impact when the tactic catches the other person off-guard: i.e., when he sees himself as an equal, or when his behavior asks that we treat him as an individual person and we treat him as an object. In either case, he feels the need to defend his concept of himself and the relationship—he becomes defensive. We have "put him down" and so he now must focus on himself to protect himself. His attention is diverted from me and us, to him solely.

Defensiveness breeds defensiveness. Openness breeds openness. Disclosure breeds disclosure (Gibb, 1961). If who we are and how we look at ourselves is partially a function of how we relate with others, then certainly, if we are defensive, the "who we are" will be significantly different than if we are open and honest when we talk with others in developing relationships.

WAYS TO OVERCOME THE MYTH

1. Develop an attitude of openness in your message sending. You know more about yourself, experiences and emotions than others. They can know you only as much as you choose to let them know you. If you want to develop relationships with other people so that they can know you and understand you, you need to let them have specific information about you.

2. Develop an attitude of disclosure in your message sending with people who you care about. In deepening, intimate relationships, knowledge of the emotional state of each participant becomes crucial to creating communication-states. What we feel is important, particularly what we feel about each other and

what we feel about the activities we are sharing. But disclosure helps relationships only if there is honesty—the willingness to tell the truth about what you feel. If you feel anger, say so; fear, say so; anxiety, say so. Once we both know what we feel we can deal with the emotions—together.

3. Select a partner. Mutually agree to discuss some topic that is controversial. Practice being open with one another. Particularly, practice being specific in reference to whose opinion it is; what it is about; its location in time and place; and the presentation of behavioral evidence. You will each probably feel uncomfortable as you try to be obviously open. Disclose to your partner your feelings—how you feel about talking openly, how you feel toward your partner.

4. The next time you feel emotional pressure (either love or anxiety) take the time to write yourself a letter in which you disclose the emotions you are feeling. Put the letter away for at least 72 hours and then read it. Could you have told others your emotions and their intensity when you were feeling them? Why not? Seek out the person(s) who were involved in the moment of emotional pressure. Show them your letter. Ask them if they knew you felt the way described. How did they feel? How do you each feel about talking about your feelings?

5. Practice identifying the emotional state of those around you when they are experiencing intense emotions. Ginott (1965) suggests we act as an "emotional mirror" to reflect back to others the emotions they are experiencing. In this way we can help the other identify and deal with his emotional state. For example, "You seem to be angry," "You appear frightened," "I sense you are uncomfortable." Practice mirroring back to others their emotional state.

a. You can practice emotional mirroring in the quiet of your own room. As you read for pleasure—novels, short stories, even magazine and newspaper human interest stories—attempt to (a) specify the emotion being felt and (b) explain the emotion in a descriptive way without judging whether the emotion is good/bad or justified/not justified.

6. Create a speech in which you practice openness and disclosure. Take a belief that is important to you. Build a speech upon the belief in which you indicate how the belief developed, why you believe, how the belief affects your communication behavior, how it affects your life. The objective is for the audience to know more about you when you have finished your speech than they knew before. The objective is not to convince your listeners to believe as you do, only to know you better.

SUMMARY

There exists a belief in our society which recommends that we should say nothing to others unless the statement is "nice." As long as we hold this belief, we prevent others from knowing us and from knowing about themselves, all of which works against our developing a meaningful relationship. Open messages contain personalized information which the listener is unlikely to know if the speaker does not tell him. In order to improve our ability to send and receive open messages we need to determine (1) *whose* opinion is being expressed, (2) *what* is being expressed, (3) *when* is the expression relevant, and (4) *why* was the expression transmitted. As a general rule we ought to be open when we have the time and energy to be understood by others.

A subset of openness is self-disclosure, the revealing of emotions as they are felt. Disclosure is important in the development of relationships because the emotions we feel help to describe our uniqueness, our individuality. Others can know us only to the extent that we tell them what we feel. In this sense, disclosure becomes important to the development of our own self-concept. Our concept grows through the reactions of others to us. If we show them a "false face" and "false emotional states" then they are not responding to us, but to some mask. The result is a distortion of the self and a weakening of the relationship. Honesty is necessary to disclosure.

When should we disclose? Self-disclosure is important when (a) we are attempting to build person-to-person relationships and (b) when we expect the relationship to deepen. People fear disclosure because our culture equates disclosure with weakness and because our culture rewards the lie. People fear disclosure also because they fear intimacy, fear taking responsibility for another, fear knowing themselves and fear the "reverse halo" effect. Finally, we suggested ways to overcome the myth, to develop attitudes of openness and disclosure with people who you care about.

7

DYADIC RELATIONSHIPS

MYTH
*"I'll Love You 'Til
the Twelfth of Never."*

While driving under an expressway overpass my wife noticed a number of expressions written with spray paint. One of them read, "Jeff and Ann Forever." We expressed anger at the selfishness of those who deface the environment. Then laughed as we recalled our own naivete when we first married—thinking that we would live together in blissful unchanging contentment until the twelfth of never. Not that we are not happy. But we have since found that relationships change as people change. Change places a great burden on the two people who want to stay in love within the context of a "dyadic relationship."

Believers in the myth act in another, seemingly opposite, way. Instead of believing that they will singly love forever, these others believe they can love anyone and everyone. I have an advisee who is openly promiscuous because she says she is "into people." She sees sexual relations as a sign of emotional relationship, as a sign of a communication-state. What she doesn't understand (and this doesn't have to be female) is that her behavior prevents the development of a communication-state and relationship. Why? She treats everyone the same (balls with all) so does not recognize the uniqueness of the other. She imposes the relationship rules of physical activity on every

155

partner ("they work"), and confuses tactile contact for intimacy. This woman doesn't understand that relationships come from working together to create something unique to the two of you and that creation is enhanced and beautiful to the extent that it reflects the uniqueness of each partner as shared through communication. She believes the myth and so fails to find, or create, the type of relationship she so eagerly seeks with others.

Who we are is a function of our interpersonal relationships, so the kinds of relationships we build and how we build them take on tremendous significance. Let us now look at dyadic relationships and by identifying their characteristics, see their importance to our individuality, how the capacity to reach a communication-state is maximized in the dyad, and why this capacity is beneficial to us as individuals trying to cope with reality and lead satisfying lives.

THE DYAD

The smallest social unit, a dyad, is the minimum number needed for a state of communication to be reached. Man does not communicate (share understanding) with himself. He communicates with someone else, if at all. The study of communication is the study of how two or more separate information-processing units come to realize they are understood and understand the other.

In a dyad, there are only three elements to analyze: each individual separately, and the relationship itself. As the number of persons in the group increases arithmetically (from two to three, four, five or more) the number of possible relationships within the group increases geometrically. For instance, in a dyad all that need be analyzed are persons A and B and the relationship A–B. But in a triad, the three persons, A, B, and C plus the dyadic relations A–B, A–C, and B–C, as well as the triadic relation A–B–C all need to be identified and studied to describe and explain their message behavior.

Some authors (Homans, 1961; Thibaut and Kelley, 1959) assume that generalizations based on studies of the dyad can apply equally well to larger social systems. This assumption is questionable. We contend that the dyad is both quantitatively and qualitatively different from other social groups: generalizations made about dyadic relationships may not necessarily be valid or as important in larger group relationships.

QUALITIES OF THE DYAD

George Simmel (1950) argues that the dyad differs quantitatively as well as qualitatively from other social units. He suggests three structural distinctions which in turn uniquely affect the interpretations of the individuals in the dyad, making the dyad a qualitatively different social system. Interestingly enough, the three structural characteristics are all absence properties: i.e., properties that characterize groups of three or more that are not prevalent in dyads.

The three structural absences mentioned are: (a) absence of potential immortality; (b) absence of specific delegation of duties and responsibilities; (c) absence of coalition formation. There are also two interpretative effects, called triviality and intimacy. We will discuss each of these distinguishing characteristics of dyads in turn.

The Absence Of Potential Immortality

A group is an identifiable social system, regardless of which persons make up its membership. The United States does not need me to be considered a nation; the Oak Park Ladies Bridge Club does not need any particular lady to remain a group. Members come in and out of these groups, playing different roles and performing various functions. Members are, then, interchangeable.

The existence of a dyad, however, is directly dependent upon each of its two members. If one party should leave, that dyad, as an identifiable group, no longer exists. For instance, suppose someone has married, divorced and then remarried. One spouse has not been exchanged for another. Instead, the first marital relationship is dead, and a brand-new interpersonal relationship has been created. There may be similarities between

157

the first and the second marriages, but, the "group" per se is a brand-new group, unique unto itself.

> A dyad, . . . depends on each of its two elements alone—in its death, though not in its life: for its life it needs *both*, but for its death, only one. This fact is bound to influence the inner attitude of the individual toward the dyad, even though not al- ways consciously nor in the same way. It makes the dyad into a group that feels itself both endangered and irreplaceable. (Simmel, 1950, p. 124)

Feelings of endangeredness or irreplaceableness are com- monly reflected in phrases like "I can't live without you," and beliefs like, "There is one and only one person in the world for me," which emphasize the uniqueness of each dyadic relation- ship. The existence of the dyad is dependent upon both of the two participants. This awareness makes each person conscious of his/her responsibility in developing and maintaining the type of interpersonal relationship they both desire. The awareness of this mutual dependency makes thoughts about the dyad's ex- istence and termination more frequent.

The death of a spouse or a divorce is not a situation where one person leaves a group to find another—as is true of changing jobs, schools, social clubs, PTAs, etc.—rather, it is a life-style change that literally requires the remaining spouse or the divorced person to re-define who he/she is. Being widowed, getting divorced or losing a close friend means that the part of a person which was wrapped in the relationship with a particular other is now cut off, dead. A person doesn't go out and simply find someone to replace the other; rather, he must build a new relationship with another. To do so, he must re-define himself to himself, in terms of the new partner. Thus, dyadic relations are indeed endangered and fragile things which must be con- tinually negotiated and worked on in order to be maintained and developed.

The Absence Of Specifically Delegated Duties And Responsibilities

A critical area of negotiation in dyadic situations is who should do what to whom, in which situations. Rules of interaction and coordination must be worked out and agreed upon, whether consciously or not. These rules concern who has the right to define the dyadic relationship and the pair's subsequent behaviors in particular situations. For instance, a wife may be able to contradict and argue with her husband when they're alone, but not in public or in front of the children. She, in turn, may have the responsibility of running the household and keeping the budget. The husband's main tasks around the house may be earning the money, taking out the garbage, and mowing the lawn. The negotiation of these acceptable behaviors and the specification of responsibilities are worked out within each particular dyad. Each and every pair must establish its own way of doing things (quid pro quo) which represents their unwritten and largely unconscious set of rules for how they should behave with each other (Lederer and Jackson, 1968, p. 179).

> Once the *quid pro quo* pattern has been established and *accepted* (no matter how bizarre the exchanges are), each partner can live from day to day with some sense of security because he knows what to expect from the other partner. Each has tacitly agreed to a behavior complex which he believes protects his own dignity, self-respect, and self-esteem in relation to the other party. Whether the actions are cruel or loving is irrelevant; both partners accept them, once the pattern is established.
> (Lederer and Jackson, 1968, p. 180)

When people exchange messages in larger social units, however, the negotiation of those quid pro quos is not as significant or prevalent, because they tend to be determined by the persons' positions or roles. The delegation and assignment of specific behaviors and responsibilities which must be performed, and for which people are held accountable is probably the most consistent feature of organized social systems. Once assigned or assumed, these behaviors and responsibilities become formal prescriptions for an individual. One's behavior is reinforced and monitored by the group's hierarchy and the group shares the responsibility for the consequences of the individuals.

The sharing of responsibility and/or blame for one's actions within the group may lead to positive and more constructive acts by the individuals. It may also induce one to commit acts which, as a separate individual, one would not commit, e.g.: kill in war. The individual at war truthfully can say, "It's not me that's doing the killing; the nation and the government are." In the same vein, the foreman who must fire a worker can tell himself that he's not hurting another individual, but is only doing his job.

I personally experienced an example of this phenomenon while I was an assistant personnel manager. On a Wednesday, I was ordered to hire forty people to start work by the following Monday. Although I thought this assignment was a bit unrealistic, much to my surprise by Friday I had forty new employees. However, on Friday at 3 p.m., I was told to fire thirty of the forty people I had just hired, because a mistake had been made in the number of new employees needed. I would not break this kind of commitment to another individual; but, because it was part of my job, I called back thirty persons and told them they were not needed and should not report for work on Monday. As an individual, I could not have done that, but as a member of an organization, just doing his job, I could and did stop thirty people from reporting to work. After all, I was just doing my job and was not responsible for the decision; the organization and its leaders were.

INSIGHT 7.1 From "The Eichmann Experiment," an interview with Stanley Milgrim, by Phillip Nobile*

Americans like to think they are better than the citizens of other countries. Professor Stanley Milgrim, of the City College of New York, sees most of us as potential concentration camp guards.

Let me describe Milgrim's so-called "Eichmann experiment." In his former laboratory at Yale, he devised an ingenious situation to test the limits of obedience. Volunteers from all walks of life were asked to participate in a memory experiment. They were instructed by a teacher to administer electric shocks to a third party whenever he came up with a wrong answer.

The shock increased in severity with the number of incorrect responses. Although the "victim" was strapped in an electric chair and screamed for mercy, a majority of the volunteers followed the orders of the teacher and pressed the last switch (450 volts) marked "Danger: Severe Shock."

160

Of course Milgrim was kidding with the shocks and the third party deserved an Oscar for his performance. Milgrim was really testing for obedience to authority. In his study by the same title, we Americans, sadly, score rather high.

Q: Are we a nation of closet Eichmanns?

A: I used to wonder whether there were sufficient moral imbeciles in the United States to man a system of death camps. After doing my experiments, I'm convinced I could recruit the necessary personnel in any medium-sized town.

*Phillip Nobile, "The Eichmann Experiment," *The State Journal,* 10 March, 1974, p. E-2.

In the dyad, however, there is no collection of others, no authority figure, to blame or praise for one's actions. Instead, each person is immediately dependent only upon the other. The direct co-responsibility for individual actions, as well as the group's actions, is more acutely felt.

> Neither of the two members can hide what he has done behind the group, nor hold the group responsible for what he has failed to do. Here, the forces with which the group surpasses the individual—indefinitely and partially, to be sure, but yet quite perceptively—cannot compensate for individual inadequacies, as they can in larger groups.
> (Simmel, 1950, p. 134)

In dyadic interpersonal situations, there is no indefineable "they" whom one can blame for one's actions. Of course, the other person in the dyad can be cited as the cause of your actions, but the other's comeback can always be (and often is) that you were the cause of his behavior. For example, the husband blames his withdrawal and inactivity on his wife's nagging. The wife, on the other hand, nags and needles him to get him out of his withdrawal and passivity. Each believes they are only reacting to the other, rather than acting upon their perceptions of the other. Each believes that he or she has no influence over what the other does. Both the husband and wife are forgetting that they are mutually responsible for what transpires between them and for what they do or fail to do.

161

In a dyad, one cannot go along for the sake of the group. One can, of course, go along for the sake of the other, and essentially, deny his right to determine what the dyad will do and become. But an emphasis on "going along for the sake of" encourages coercive and manipulative behavior within the dyad and discourages open, honest expressions of feelings, wants and perceptions. Rather than negotiating and sharing each others' feelings and desires, and working out a satisfactory quid pro quo, an all-or-nothing strategy can quickly develop in the dyad: "If you don't take me to the dance, I'll never go out with you again," or "If you don't take me to the movie, I won't sleep with you tonight," or "If you don't eat your spinach, you can't go out to play after dinner." In other words, the implicit command is "Either you do it my way, or you get nothing at all." This all-or-nothing strategy is much more frequently seen in dyadic situations than in group relations. Groups stress compromise and collaboration, while dyads stress personalized bargaining. In groups, the control dimensions of the relationship are not so visible and the bargaining not so personalized.

The Absence Of Possible Coalition Formation

In groups of three or more, there is always the possibility, if not the probability, that a majority will get together and overrule the individual. Two or more persons can form a coalition to override the other and dominate the decision.* The mother and daughter can "gang-up" on Dad in order to get a new dress for the daughter's prom. The secretaries can agree to process the forms any way they want until the boss changes his mind to adopt their ideas. Two roommates can decide not to clean the room until the third roommate starts doing her part in keeping the room clean and presentable. The tendency for groups to form coalitions to overrule another group is the basis for the oft-quoted phrase: "Politics makes for strange bedfellows," which emphasizes the necessity of forming temporary power coalitions to bring about some change or stop some proposal.

---

*See Caplow, 1968, and Gamson, 1961, for an analysis of coalition formation.

162

In a dyad, however, there can be no majority formed to overrule and outvote a minority. There is only one person dominating and another submitting or both persons getting their act together and working out their own unique relational rules. Between the two people, there is no other to help support one side; there are just the two deciding what should be done, how and when. The husband cannot appeal to his boss for support for his position that the wife should do the grocery shopping. Legitimately, there is just he and his wife. The wife cannot fairly appeal to her teacher for support of her desire to go on and get her degree in astronomy. Just she and her husband must decide. The violation of this "just the two of us" notion by bringing in outside support is often considered "dirty pool" by the other person. He/she feels that the one bringing in outside support is not "playing by the rules." Indeed, the relational rules have been broken! When a third person is brought in to support one person's point-of-view, there are no longer two persons, alone, facing the issue: there is one versus two. The impossibility of forming coalitions of two against one, emphasize the co-responsibility for behaviors in the dyad.

HEIGHTENED INDIVIDUALITY

In larger social units (with potential immortality) which delegate duties and responsibilities, and in which an individual can be overruled and outvoted, the tendency is toward devaluation of the individual. The absence of these three characteristics highlights individuality in dyad relations. Any particular individual's unique contribution, responsibility, and significance decrease rapidly as the size of the group increases. For instance, think for a moment about your own experiences. You, as an acting, responsible free individual are constantly involved in decisions about what you and one other will do. You may be heavily involved in decisions in groups of three, four or five, but your involvement will probably be less. In a classroom, your own unique actions are relatively less significant in terms of their effects on the climate and decisions of the class: your own presence or absence may not even be felt by your classmates. In a large organization, your individual actions are constrained and your own thoughts have little effect on what you do and how you do it. In other words, on a continuum of individuation-to-de-individuation, the two-person social unit allows for the most individuality, sense of personal significance, and personal freedom and responsibility.

INCREASED PERSONAL RESPONSIBILITY

The most personal responsibility and involvement is felt in dyadic relationships. This increased sense of responsibility and involvement makes satisfactory dyadic relations important for each individual's sense of self-worth and self-esteem. For instance, don't you feel on top of the world when you and your date (or spouse) are getting along well? It doesn't matter if other things aren't going too well. Knowing that there is at least one other person who accepts and appreciates you, puts you "on top of the world" (as the Carpenters sing it). The reverse is also felt, so that if you are not getting along with your date, or roommate, or spouse, it doesn't matter that everything else is going smoothly—'cause, damn it! the one you are most involved with doesn't seem to accept and appreciate your uniqueness. Your own sense of worth and self-esteem are very much involved in the relationship with that one other (whether it be a roommate, a fiancee, a wife, a friend, or whoever) and when that's not going well, you don't feel "good" about yourself.

Another effect of this relatively greater sense of responsibility, freedom and individuality felt in dyads is the presumption that the group will not lower the individual person to some average level. The dyad is less dependent upon average qualities for its typical performance level, and is more dependent upon individual qualities. For example, the members of a group can move only as fast as the slowest persons. In a classroom, the odds are that each student will get bored and tired once in awhile, because information that he comprehends must be repeated for others. In a small group meeting, it often seems that some points are repeated and rehashed interminably because someone doesn't understand, or wasn't listening, or

164

doesn't want to pay attention. The group's performance as a whole is geared to, and determined by, the average qualities of its members. In a dyadic situation, on the other hand, the behaviors of the two are relatively less dependent on the average qualities of the members and are more heavily dependent upon the *unique* characteristics of each person. Thus, in Simmel's words, "basically anything larger than two tends to de-individualize and specialize."

In groups of three or more, each person will feel less involved and less committed to the group, since he knows that he can, and must, give only parts of himself to the group. The only part of self needed and wanted by the group is that part which plays the role of group member. Playing a social role is neither phony nor a "put-on"—it is simply a limited part of any individual's self. When I am playing teacher, only part of me is involved in that role. This de-personalization of social and organizational roles allows for interchangeability of people, or parts, within the organization. In the dyad, however, the very existence of the unit is directly and immediately dependent upon the uniqueness of each individual.

INTERPRETATIVE QUALITIES OF THE DYAD

Triviality

One of the interpretative characteristics made relatively more important in dyadic situations as a result of the absence of structural properties is triviality. Judgments about triviality arise from feelings of being "endangered and irreplaceable." Triviality is a frequency notion focusing on how many times the behavior, message, or circumstance has happened before for the individual. Given our heightened sense of individuality in dyadic relations, we want and need to have our uniqueness, our individuality, recognized and affirmed by the other. If we feel we are not being treated as a unique person, we may judge our actions with the other as trivial.

"Triviality" connotes a certain measure of frequency, of the consciousness that a content of life is repeated, while the value of this content depends on its very opposite—a certain measure of rarity.

(Simmel, 1950, p. 125)

Simmel suggests that this measure of triviality is less operative in larger social units because the individual knows he is replaceable. Being a teacher or personnel manager, joining a sorority, playing on an athletic team, being in a college speech course, may all be unique for the individual, but they are not unique to him. However, where interpersonal exchange is immediately tied to the direct contribution of each individual— where each shares equal responsibility for what happens—concerns for one's uniqueness, for one's individual significance, are relatively more important. If a person feels he/she is being treated the way several others were previously treated by the other person, then the relationship may be judged to be trivial.

The classic example of this feeling is the smooth-talking ladies' man who has a "line a mile long." Ordinarily a girl would feel valued if her own uniqueness, her own individual strengths, beauty, and talents were being praised. She would believe herself an important, attractive and worthwhile person. However, in the case of a ladies' man, a girl may not realize that he is simply repeating an oft-rehearsed set of phrases for a particular result. She is not being praised; their immediate relationship is not being valued. Rather, she is being manipulated by a standard set of behaviors which give the appearance of concern and admiration for her. If she were to see through the "line," she would realize that the messages and behaviors have little respect or concern for her as an individual, but rather emphasize her existence as an object to be exploited and used.

INSIGHT 7.2   From *Man the Manipulator* by Everett L. Shostrom*

Modern man is a manipulator.

· · · · · ·

The manipulator is legion. He is all of us, consciously, subconsciously, or unconsciously employing all the phony tricks we absorb between the cradle and grave to conceal the actual vital nature of ourselves and, in the process, reducing ourselves and our fellow man into things to be controlled.

Not all our manipulating is evil of course, and some of it appears necessary in the competitive arena of earning a livelihood. Much, however, is quite harmful since it masks real illness which can erupt in shattered lives, broken marriages and ruined careers. To the humanistic psychologist it is tragedy enough that modern man by his manipulating seems to have lost all his spontaneity, all capacity to feel and express himself directly and creatively, thus debasing himself into an anxious automaton who wastes his hours trying to recapture the past and insure the future. Oh, he talks about his feelings, but he rarely experiences them. He is, in fact, very glib at talking of his troubles and generally quite bad at coping with them, reducing life to a series of verbal and intellectual exercises and drowning himself in a sea of words. He gropes along under a wardrobe of masks and concealing statements, unaware of the real richness of being.

. . . A *manipulator* may be defined as a person who exploits, uses and/or controls himself and others as things in certain self-defeating ways. While every man is to some degree a manipulator (I confess), modern humanistic psychology suggests that out of these manipulations we can develop positive potential which Abraham Maslow and Kurt Goldstein call "self-actualizing." The opposite of the manipulator is the *actualizor* (a rare bird in pure form) who may be defined as a person who appreciates himself and his fellow man as persons or subjects with unique potential—an expressor of his actual self. The paradox is that each of us is partly a manipulator and partly an actualizor, but we can continually become more actualizing.

A person who is *actualizing* trusts his feelings, communicates his needs and preferences, admits to desires and misbehaviors, enjoys a worthy foe, offers real help when needed, and is, among many other things, honestly and constructively aggressive. The manipulator, on the other hand, habitually conceals and camouflages his real feelings behind a repertoire of behavior which runs the scale from arrogant hostility to servile flattery in his continuous campaign to serve his own wishes. In part, at least, he is a manipulator because he isn't aware of his actualizing potential . . .

* From *Man, the Manipulator,* by Everett Shostrom. Copyright © 1967 by Abingdon Press.

Many of our present-day interpersonal encounters are manipulative and impersonal in nature and people are viewed as things to be used, says Shostrom (1967). The salesman sees the person as a customer; the barber sees the person as a head of hair; the gas station attendant claims he can be very friendly, not because you are you, but because he needs your regular visits; the politician sees you as a potential vote; the teacher sees you as a state of ignorance that must be ameliorated; the clergyman views you as another soul to save. In these situations, only part of ourselves is being perceived and appreciated—the part that the other wants to use or exploit. The continual, proper and convincing playing of roles, of presenting only those parts of ourselves that we have in common with others, may not, in itself, be trivial. But when those persons with whom we have the opportunity to share ourselves become simply another object to be treated like other objects in our environment—that is trivial. When the uniqueness of each individual is not shared, developed, and appreciated, when our own individuality is not understood and allowed to be expressed—that is trivial.

> Americans thus find themselves in a vicious circle, in which their extrafamilial relationships are increasingly arduous, competitive, trivial and irksome, in part as a result of efforts to avoid or minimize potentially irksome or competitive relationships. As the few vestiges of stable and familiar community life erode, the desire for a simple, cooperative life style grows in intensity. The most seductive appeal of radical ideologies for Americans consists in the fact that all in one way or another attack the competitive foundations of our society.
> (Slater, 1970, p. 10)

The result of being in continually trivial relationships is an increase in our desire for interpersonal intimacy, for the creation of interpersonal relations where both persons are free to control and be controlled.

Intimacy

Although some degree of intimacy can be obtained and felt in groups, it reaches its highest levels in dyadic transactions. "The larger the group is, the more easily does it form an objective unit up and above its members, and the less intimate does it become; the two characteristics are intrinsically connected" (Simmel, 1950, p. 127). The feeling of intimacy stems from the sharing of one's uniqueness. The more two persons share their own unique perceptions, dreams, hopes, fears, skills, and experiences with only one other, the more intimate the relationship becomes.

168

One can share personal information with another (i.e., express open messages and self-disclosure), but that does not make the relationship intimate. Rather, an intimate relationship is based on those experiences, concerns, perceptions, behaviors, and feelings that one shares exclusively with another. Again, to use Simmel's words, the relationship is an intimate one . . .

. . . if its whole affective structure is based on what each of the two participants gives or shows only to the one other person and to nobody else. In other words, intimacy is not based on the *content* of the relationship.
(Simmel, 1950, pp. 126-127).

INSIGHT 7.3 From *Pairing* by Dr. George R. Bach and Ronald M. Deutsch*

Why does today's psychologist see intimate love as so important? Because what men and women seek from love today is no longer a romantic luxury; it is an essential of emotional survival. Less and less it is a hunt for the excitement of infatuation, or for the doubtful security of the marriage nest. More and more it is the hope of finding in intimate love something of personal validity, personal relevance, a confirmation of one's existence.

For in today's world, when men and women are made to feel as faceless as numbers on a list, they want intimate love to provide the feelings of worth and identity that preserve sanity and meaning. They hunger for one pair of eyes to give them true recognition and acceptance, for one heart that understands and can be understood. Only genuine intimacy satisfies these hungers.

When the quest for intimacy fails, personality is endangered. Those who fail tend to blame themselves, and to doubt their adequacy as men and women. They develop self-images of being cold, unfeeling, selfish, perhaps incapable of mature love and so doomed to inner isolation.

* Dr. George R. Bach and Ronald M. Deutsch, *Pairing* (New York: Avon Books, 1970), pp. 14-15.

Even though intimacy is not based on the content of the messages exchanged, intimacy cannot be established without the exchange of self-disclosing, open and honest expressions. But, just because these messages have been transmitted does not mean the relationship is an intimate one. For instance, research has shown that people tend to self-disclose most to friends, somewhat less to strangers and least to acquaintances. None of us would claim that an intimate relationship had been created with a stranger on the plane, on the bus, at the campground, or in a distant bar. These might have been warm, personally rewarding times of interpersonal sharing, and beautiful experiences, but they were not intimate relationships. For intimacy to develop, there must be sustained interactions that involve risks and trust. The two persons' feelings about each other and about themselves become enmeshed in the "whole affective structure" of their relationship. Personal validation, acceptance and feelings of self-worth all become dependent upon what the two people do and share together: that is intimacy. It requires risk, trust, knowledge of the other, and a willingness to become dependent upon the other person and the relationship.

This highly exclusive sharing of one's self with another is a primary source of personal confirmation and acceptance and may help one to develop emotional stability. But, this sharing must be sustained in order for the relationship to last. Every interpersonal relationship is a process, a continual cycle of growth, decay, re-development, stagnation, death—in a word, change. These ever-present changes, no matter how minimal they seem, require that the dyad constantly work at their relationship if they are to maintain themselves and grow. Quoting Powell:

> Friendship and mutual self-revelation have a newness about them with each new day, because being a human person involves daily change and growth. My friend and I are growing, and differences are becoming more apparent. We are not growing into the same person, but each into his own. I discover my friend's other tastes and preferences, other feelings and hopes, other reactions to new experiences. I discover that this business of telling him who I am cannot be done once and for all. I must *continually* tell you who I am and you must *continually* tell me who you are, because both of us are continually evolving.
> (Powell, 1969, pp. 98–99)

If personal and relational changes are not worked at and included in the dyad's transactions, then the things two people have shared may become a source of triviality and relational decay within the dyad. Also, if two people concentrate only on those behaviors and feelings they exclusively share, then the relationship may come to be judged as trivial. For instance, Betty and Dick were both education majors who got married and were working their way through school. Initally, they were very happy, and things were moving along well. Over time, however, Betty became intrigued with microbiology, and Dick decided to become a sociology major. They did not share their new interests with each other. "Well, he/she would not be interested," they politely convinced themselves, not wanting to bore the other. Pretty soon, Betty was spending more and more time in the lab, while Dick was at the library and social demonstrations. They didn't really notice that they were not spending as much time together, even though they were living under the same roof. The reason? "Well, I've been too busy, and he/she doesn't want to listen to this stuff, anyway." Social affairs quickly became a nuisance and they seldom went out together, because "Well, he/she doesn't like the same people I do." Although they still did things together—they had always enjoyed swimming, hiking and camping—they didn't feel like they were together. "You're not the same person I married," they'd accusingly tell each other, partly worried and partly confused. Right! They were not the same people they'd married. They'd changed, and hadn't allowed those changes to be included in their relationship. With good intentions, they'd politely not allowed those changes to be shared with the other. By not working at their relationship, they'd lost it, and are now divorced and at different schools.

If a dyad concentrates solely on those matters which they exclusively share (not including their interests, hopes, and perceptions about other matters, which may be objectively more important), they run the risk of making their relationship trivial. Over time, the dyad's members may conclude that the talents, skills, and experiences which each most constructively has to offer, lie outside their relationship and their intimacy may become a source of triviality. This result is possible in any long-term personal encounter, but may be particularly likely in marriage where relatively more "heavy" intellectual, political and/or ethical concerns are discussed with others and not with one's spouse. "After all, he/she knows how I feel," people will say confidently. How? By divine inspiration?

The parts of self which are shared with others but are not part of that which the two solely give to each other are excluded from the dyad's interactions. This exclusion may lead to a gradual decline in the significance of the relationship to the individuals and to eventual heartache, mistrust, misunderstanding, break-up or divorce. Why? Partly because the two forget that they are a process and that reaching a communication-state is hard work which must be continually re-accomplished. They are unwilling or unable to share with the other, and forget their own individual responsibility for determining the nature of their relationship.

Good intentions are not enough—responsible behavior, showing concern for the other, is what counts. What you do with others, how you behave towards them and with them, the kinds of relationships you develop, determines your own self-concept, the concept of the other, and ultimately determines the kind of society we will live in. Think about what you do to others. Be concerned with how you behave with them.

Even though the behaviors suggested in this book cannot assure more satisfying and rewarding relationships, they can move all of us in that direction. The alternative is to continue to believe the myths we have identified and to accept the alienation, self-deprecation, exploitation and defensiveness existing all around us.

WAYS TO OVERCOME THE MYTH

1. Develop an attitude of impermanence toward the relationship. This may sound negative, but it isn't. If you begin to think of the relationship as impermanent, that you might lose the other and so lose yourself through the loss of the relationship, extra effort may be exerted to keep the relationship. Not keep it "as it is" but keep the feelings between two people growing and changing as they grow and change.

2. Express your uniqueness and let others express theirs. Which means be open in the messages you send and be willing

172

to risk self-disclosure with those people you wish to develop a relationship. You cannot find the other, nor the other you, nor can you mutually establish the rule for the relationship if you are not open or fail to disclose. In so doing you help to overcome the tendency toward triviality as discussed in the chapter. And you engage in intimacy the sharing of experiences exclusively with another. From openness and disclosure to reduced triviality and enhanced intimacy you have established conditions for a communication-state to be developed. So long as you and your partner hide, not accepting responsibility for the relationship, the less the chance for mutual understanding.

3. The next time you converse with a loved one notice how "trivial" is your talk. Do you talk about topics which you talk about with others? In the same way? Using the same words and gestures? Once you've left the conversation record the same conversation but in a way which reflects the uniqueness of the other person and the relationship the two of you share. This can be done in a journal. Or, after writing, re-converse with your partner. Then tell your dyadic partner what and why you are re-conversing about the topic.

SUMMARY

We identified a myth in our culture which says that relationships can go on forever unchanged and that we can have a meaningful relationship with anyone. Neither belief is correct. In dispelling the myth we attempted to show that the characteristics of a dyad, impermanence, mutually agreed upon rules, and the impossibility of power coalitions developing, encourage and depend upon the expression of uniqueness of the individual within the relationship. Assuming that one can love forever or that anyone can have a meaningful relationship denies this fundamental point of uniqueness. We also argued that expending energy within a relationship heightens the individuality of a person—you find yourself in the dyad, you don't lose yourself. Why? Because only with one other can you express *you*. We also

173

noted that with increased individuality comes increased responsibility for the other. The more you two work together the more responsible you become for the other and the other for you. Finally we pointed out that dyadic relationships encourage open expression and self-disclosure. To send other kinds of messages is trivial and undercuts the importance and uniqueness of the dyad as well as denies intimacy. We then suggested some attitude changes which will help us overcome the myth.

8

TRUST
AND CONTROL
IN RELATIONSHIPS

MYTH
*"Me? I Don't
Influence Anybody."*

The following conversation between a guy and a girl was overheard recently at the beach:

He: (decisively) "You know that inflatable boat of yours that I've blown up so many times, I'm finally going to go for a ride in it."

She: (enthusiastically) "Oh good. You can take me for a ride."

He: (kiddingly but firmly) "No. I will not *take* you for a ride, Turkey. If you want to come along, great. I would like for us to go out together, but I won't *take* you for a ride."

She: (hurt and sad) "No, that's okay. You go out by yourself. I'll stay here and sunbathe."

He: (firmly but apologetically) "Come on, Sweetie. Don't be hurt. Let's go for a ride."

She: (hurt and retreating) "No, that's okay. I'll just . . ."

He: (getting frustrated) "Come on. Let's go for a ride. I want you to come." (ordering but pleading) "Now, get in the boat."

She: (getting in the boat, but still sad) "When you said you were going out, I just wanted to be with you. I thought it would be fun."

He: (firmly but warmly) "I know you wanted to be included, Honey. But, I wanted you to know that I would not be your slave and *take* you for a ride. I like to do things *with* you, but I don't like feeling as if I'm being ordered to do things for you." (lightly and smilingly) "Now, let's go for that ride!"

What's this conversation all about? Certainly not about a boat ride, even though that is the content of the messages. The conversation is about who has the right to control the couple's actions. The man interpreted the woman's comment as an order, an attempt to dictate what he should do. He rejected the order, but accepted the idea of going out together. The woman, in turn, stated she didn't mean it as an order, but just as expression of her desire for them to play together. They seemed to straighten out the disagreement, and looked as if they were going to enjoy their boat ride. They realized that they each influence the other; that they both are responsible for what they do and become.

TRUST DIMENSION IN TRANSACTION

Exchanging messages and reaching a communication-state are mutual activities, which have reciprocal effects on the persons interacting. The process of communicating is a transactional one. A transactional perspective emphasizes that the relationship of the speaker and listener is both a consequence and a determinant of who will transmit what information in which situations. One major characteristic of this transactional relationship is *trust*. Distrusts and suspicion of another's intentions tend to increase defensiveness and decrease the frequency of honest open expressions, thereby decreasing mutual understanding and the likelihood of sharing meaning. The trust dimension of interpersonal relationships, in other words, is concerned with the way in which each person judges the intentions of the other when deciding how to behave with him.

INSIGHT 8.1   From *Caring Enough to Confront* by David Augsburger*

To be trusted, you must trust. To receive trust from others, you risk trusting them by opening yourself to them. These two go together—trust and openness.

A climate of mutual trust develops out of mutual freedom to express real feelings, positive and negative. As each person moves toward a greater acceptance of his total self, more and more of his/her potential for loving, trusting, responsibility, and growth are released.

And as the trust level rises between parent and child, the willingness to be open with each other increases too. The two go hand in hand. Trust and openness. Acceptance and honesty. Love and risk.

There are risks involved in all love, acceptance, and trust. If I come to understand another's inner world; if I can sense his confusion or his timidity, or his feeling of being treated unfairly; if I can feel it as if it were my own, then a highly sensitive empathy comes into play between us. A rare kind of trusting-understanding develops.

This is far different from the understanding which says: "I know what's wrong with you," or "I can see what makes you act that way."

This trusting-understanding enters the other's world in his or her terms. And that is risky. If I take your world into mine, I run the risk of being changed, of becoming more like you.

* David Augsburger, *Caring Enough to Confront* (Glendale, Calif.: Regal Books Division, GL Publications, 1973), pp. 87–88.

All human relationships are based on the phenomenon of trust. Trust appears to be the most crucial dimension, the one upon which all potential and on-going relationships are evaluated. Why? Communication-states develop when two or more persons realize they understand and are understood. But due to the infinite number of subtle differences between people, no way exists for one person to make another a complete participant in his information and perceptions. Each of us has our own purposes and interpretations which make up our own unique realities. Since we can never completely comprehend and share another's reality, the best we can do is trust or distrust the other's behaviors and intentions (Watzlawick et al., 1967, p. 226). The Gibbs' maintain:

> Trust is the pacemaker variable in group growth. From it stem all other significant variables of health. That is, to the extent that trust develops, people are able to communicate genuine feelings and perceptions on relevant issues to all members of the system. (Gibb and Gibb, 1967, p. 163)

They go on to stress that the establishment of trust in interpersonal relations is crucial for individual and group growth. Only within a trusting interpersonal climate can each person be accepted, and personal acceptance is fundamental for group achievement and development.

Components: Trusting and Trustworthy Behaviors

Trust is made up of the components of trusting and trustworthy behaviors. Trust exists in a relationship if and only if these behaviors are exhibited. The level of trust between people is produced, maintained, and changed through trusting and trustworthy behaviors. The reciprocal performance of these types of behaviors forms an interlocking, self-perpetuating pattern between the persons so that trust either grows or degenerates over time.

A certain amount of trust must exist between persons if they are to reach a communication-state. The mutual sharing required for communication to occur necessitates that some degree of trust be present. Trust is said to exist in an interpersonal relationship if both persons behave in trusting and trustworthy manners. Since the degree of trust is inferred from the observed performance of trusting and trustworthy behaviors, the definitions of these behaviors are the critical elements in analyzing the amount of trust existing within a given interpersonal relationship. Let's turn now to the definitions of trusting and trustworthy behaviors. To do this, an extended example will be used to illustrate the criteria used to identify these behaviors.

Trusting behavior. Jim and Lillian have been dating for slightly more than a year. At first they both dated others, but now they go out only with each other and see each other about every day. Jim wants to be more open to Lillian about how

178

much he loves and needs her. His purpose is to reach a closer, more intimate, sharing relation with Lillian. Jim believes that one way of reaching this closer relationship is to mutually explore each other's personal feelings, fears, hopes and dreams. But, if Jim does verbally disclose his feelings to Lillian, he's afraid she might deny and laugh at his feelings, and/or think he is just using a seductive trick, and/or feel like she's being trapped into a closer relationship than she desires, and/or feel like she's being pressured into marriage which she doesn't yet want. Any or all of these interpretations could result in Lillian breaking up with Jim or at least pushing her into dating others. None of these results is desired by Jim. His intentions are to increase the depth and closeness of their relationship, but the possibility of losing Lillian is more frightening to Jim than the pleasure of honestly expressing and exploring his feelings. How then, does Jim behave? Does he take the risk or not?

This example has all the elements of trusting behavior. If Jim chooses to self-disclose, predicting that Lillian will not misunderstand him, then his openness will be considered trusting.

Trusting behavior is always unidirectional in nature, running from one person to another (from Jim to Lillian in this case). The behavior from Jim's perspective is purposeful and is intended to result in some positively valued outcome or goal. Jim realizes that in order to reach his goal, he needs Lillian and expects that she will behave in a manner consistent with his positively valued outcomes. Trusting behavior, therefore, has the following three components from Jim's perspective:

1) *The behavior has motivational relevance for Jim in that he desires some outcome to occur and does not want some other outcome(s) to result from his behaviors.* Furthermore, the negative or unwanted consequences are potentially more damaging to his situation and/or self-concept (i.e., he might lose or push Lillian away) than the positive consequences are reinforcing.

2) *The behavior has a predictability element for Jim in that he expects that the positive consequences have a greater probability of occurring than the negative consequences.* In other words, Jim expects that it is more likely for Lillian to accept his feelings than to reject them, and/or feel trapped and pressured.

179

Furthermore, he realizes that he needs Lillian's acceptance if a closer relationship is to develop.

3) *The open messages are transmitted with the intention and the expectation that the positive consequences (i.e., a closer relationship) will develop.* Jim decides to self-disclose his feelings of warmth and love.

If and only if the above three conditions are met, can some behavior or behavioral sequence be called trusting: when one observes "trusting behavior," the above three elements will always be present. These conditions appear to reflect one's intuitive meaning of the phrases "I trust . . .", "I did trust . . .", or "I have trusted . . .". In everyday language, trusting behavior is reflected in first-person statements.

Trustworthy behavior. Trustworthy behavior is likewise unidirectional. In this case, it is Lillian's behavioral response toward, with respect to and/or in conjunction with, Jim. From Lillian's perspective, her behavior is intended to aid or assist Jim in obtaining his desires and/or negate, avoid or neutralize his potential negative consequences. Furthermore, Lillian is aware that Jim is relying on and trusting her. An altruistic motivation is not required or implied: e.g., she doesn't accept Jim's statement because she pities or feels sorry for him. The only stipulation is that Lillian be aware of Jim's situation in terms of the potentially greater negative outcomes and that she in some way feel obligated to fulfill his expectations. This obligation may be based on either Lillian's awareness of Jim's confidence and reliance on her, and/or on Lillian's own reward structure. Trustworthy behavior, then, has the following three characteristics.

1) *Lillian is aware of Jim's motivational preference.* She correctly perceives that for Jim the potential negative consequences are larger than the potential positive consequences. This is not to imply that her estimates of his evaluations of the potential outcomes are equivalent, but only that Lillian is aware that the potential positive outcomes are less important than the potential negative outcomes.

2) *Lillian is aware that Jim has confidence in and is relying on her.* This awareness may be termed a feeling of obligation on

the part of Lillian. She is aware that Jim thinks the positive results are more likely than the negative outcomes if he behaves toward her in a trusting manner. Also, Lillian perceives, accurately or not, that she is in some sense being relied upon by Jim.

3) *Lillian performs those sets of behaviors that are requested by Jim, increasing the likelihood of Jim's positive outcomes,* and/or decreasing or neutralizing the possibility and the effects of the negative outcomes for Jim. Lillian, then, understands Jim's intent, accepts his expressions of warmth, and does not feel trapped or pressured by the self-disclosure. If and only if the above three elements are present, can Lillian's behavior be said to be trustworthy. In everyday statements concerning trustworthiness, these conditions are reflected in third-person statements (e.g.: "He can be trusted"; "They can be counted on"; "She was trusted"; "He can be relied on").

The condition of trust exists in a relationship, then, if both persons have mutually engaged in trusting and trustworthy behaviors with respect to each other. That is, if both parties engage in behaviors with the other that have potentially greater negative consequences than positive consequences; both need the other and expect that the other's behavior will result in those positive outcomes; and both parties behave in ways that fulfill the other's expectation and result in the positive outcomes (or at least not the negative outcomes) for the other in that situation.

INSIGHT 8.2   From *Mirages of Marriage* by William J. Lederer and Don D. Jackson*

One of the necessary ingredients of a workable marriage is trust. "Trust" is defined as "confidence in or reliance on some quality or attribute of a person or thing, or the truth of a statement." It is also defined as "the quality of being trustworthy; fidelity; loyalty; trustiness."

More immediately applicable to the marital situation are the definitions of the verb, "to trust"; "to have faith or confidence that something desired is or will be the case," and "to invest with a charge; to confide or entrust something to the care or disposal of the other."

The trouble with these definitions is that they imply that trust can be unilateral, as when the infant trusts his mother because he is tiny and she is large and he has no other choice. Trust in marriage is different. It is formed on the basis of exchanges of behavior (and hence, information) which go on all the time between spouses. When the spouses, by their behavior, are communicating clearly to each other, there is no "noise" on the line between them; then there is trust, because they read each other clearly. Each spouse can understand and accept the significance, the intent, the values, and the meanings of the other's behavioral repertoire; and if there is any doubt, he feels free to clarify the matter immediately.

Trust is not something that one or the other spouse has as a personal quality or character trait; it is present between the two if it is warranted by their exchange of behavior. Naturally, during stress, unclear communication, or confusion, the trust existing between a couple may temporarily diminish, but the experience may fortify trust over the long run if they successfully handle the situation. Thus, trust is developed over a period of time as the result of experience . . .   (pp. 106–107)

"Love, honor, and obey . . . 'till death do us part" is an unrealistic part of the Christian marriage vow because it suggests that trust is static. In the mystique of the marriage ceremony, spouses assume that by saying "I do" they have signed a rigid and unalterable pact, and therefore they *expect* trust from each other. Trust is not created by expectations. It develops as a result of mutual shared experiences which are clarified between the spouses. The Christian marital vow is based on the fallacy that nothing will change. Trust in marriage does *not* mean, "I am certain that you, my darling spouse, will always be exactly the same as I estimated you to be the day we were married." Trust is the result of a flexible, developmental bargain between spouses which endures because it is able to accommodate change. (p. 107)

Those couples who enjoy trust, who give trust to each other, probably are among the most fortunate people alive. Note that we say "couples," not "individuals." It is obvious that for trust to exist *both* spouses must be completely open and truthful with each other. This is difficult. People in our culture are taught to lie from childhood, whether their instruction is overt or implicit. Children learn that if they tell the truth (for example, comment on all that they observe, such as behavior of adults) they will be rejected or punished. Dishonesty is so greatly expected in our society that courts require witnesses to testify "under oath." Much of the training that a trial lawyer receives is intended to give him skill in exposing dishonesty on the part of those testifying. Psychiatrists know that many patients lie to them—and pay a fee for the privilege. The Internal Revenue Service is organized in the expectation of falsified income-tax returns.

Because we are reared in dishonesty (largely the dishonesty of omission, as in politeness or diplomacy), complete truthfulness is most unusual. (p. 109) . . . Trust requires the constant exercise of intelligence, truthfulness and courage. Perhaps that is why it is so rare. (p. 113)

* William J. Lederer and Don D. Jackson, "Trust in Marriage," *Mirages of Marriage* (New York: W. W. Norton & Company, Inc., 1968), pp. 106-113.

This discussion of trust suggests several things to us as potential communicators.

(1) Trust is hard to develop and very easily destroyed. The development of trust within a relationship takes time. Trust requires that both people initially take some risks, and that these risks do not result in personal harm. Open messages are said to be risky, because the information they contain can be used against you. If the information you've disclosed is used against you in some way, the level of trust that has developed is quickly shattered. For instance, suppose Jim (from our earlier example) had self-disclosed and Lillian had laughed at his feelings, calling him a fool for getting so involved. On top of this, suppose Jim finds out that Lillian has told some of her friends and is bragging about how she outsmarted him and how shy and vulnerable he is. How would Jim feel about this? He would probably be hurt, saddened and mad. He would feel his trust had been violated (and it would have been) and he might want to get revenge, and/or be certain that he'd never trust her again, and/or generalize to all women, assuring himself that he'd never again be hurt by a female. None of these results were intended, nor would they help the people learn about themselves—to grow emotionally and intellectually.

Continuing this example, let's assume that Lillian came to Jim saying that she was sorry, that she really did need him and wanted them to get back together. What would Jim be liable to think and do? Would he believe and trust her or not? What would Lillian have to do to re-establish the level of trust? Although they might get back together, it would take some time before Jim's suspicions would be quieted and the previous level of trust and warmth were re-established. If, however, Jim immediately accepted her back, assuming that the relationship was just as it had been, his behavior might be considered too trusting.

(2) A second suggestion for action is that inappropriately trusting another can be just as dysfunctional as never trusting another. People who repeatedly act in trusting manners even though there doesn't seem to be any reason for it, are commonly called "suckers" and frequently are exploited. Being overly trusting, or kind, or open, or generous with yourself, your time and possessions may be just as dysfunctional as never trusting another. Why? Because others may come to believe that you can't make responsible choices, that you don't respect yourself, that you don't care enough about yourself to be cautious and protect your own feelings and possessions. If you don't care enough about yourself, why should they? Furthermore, as paradoxical as it may sound, people who always act in a trusting manner cannot be trusted. Trust implies choice, an awareness of the risks involved. Trusting and trustworthy behavior are not expected or forced, but are given freely and intentionally. If someone seems to be unaware of the risks and is always unconditionally trusting, then others know that this person will never retaliate, can be easily exploited without fear of reprisals, and thus cannot be trusted. Blind faith (believing that others will always help and never harm you) cannot be considered trust because no choice is involved.

(3) The social situation will affect the development of trust. If the situation is perceived as a competitive one (i.e., every man for himself), then every man is likely to protect himself. Suspicion and distrust are likely to dominate. If the world is viewed as a dog-eat-dog place where what one wins another must lose, then defensiveness, threats and suspicion are likely to characterize our interpersonal relations. Incidently, Hochreich and Rotter (1970) report that there has been a small but steady decline over the last few years in the "generalized expectancy" of college students that others can be trusted. If this trend continues, as one student said, "Trust will soon go the way of the model-T Ford and this will indeed be a sad world to live in." If, one the other hand, the social situation is defined as a cooperative one where individual rewards are based on what

both persons do, then some amount of coordination and sharing is likely to occur and some degree of trust can develop. If the interdependence of personal rewards is emphasized in social situations then the likelihood of more open and honest message exchanges increases, the probability of trust development increases, and the probability of obtaining interpersonal understanding is enhanced.

Now, don't get us wrong. We are not arguing against competition. Competing for goals and rewards has many advantages. Competition encourages people to do their best, to get involved, to think about what they are doing and why. What we are arguing against is competition that is defined as a win-lose situation in which when one wins, the other must lose an equivalent amount—the other has to be beaten regardless of the cost to us in order to feel we've won. Does this sound idealistic and unrealistic? Perhaps. But what are the alternatives? To increase the level of distrust and suspicion? To increase the amount of loneliness and alienation that exists in our society? Those alternatives don't appear very desirable or realistic. Therefore, take the risk once in awhile; be trusting, make open statements and allow the other to be trustworthy. Likewise, be trustworthy and dependable. Don't intentionally take advantage of the other or harm his self-perceptions by spreading malicious gossip or betraying his confidence in you. Live up to your commitments. Your own ability to trust may increase, the level of involvement with others may be deeper and more satisfying, the chances of sharing understanding will increase, and life may be a little more fulfilling.

CONTROL DIMENSION IN TRANSACTION

The *control* aspect (sometimes discussed as power, authority, and/or influence) of an interpersonal relationship refers to who is given the right to define the situation, or, who decides what behaviors the interactants will emit. These definitions are observed in the "command" aspects of the verbal and nonverbal messages transmitted. In each and every social situation, the question is never whether or not control exists. Rather, the key question concerns who is in control of what behaviors in which situations. Going through revolving doors with another, standing in ticket lines, working on an assembly line, playing bridge, or going drinking, all require predictability and intermingling of behaviors. This blending necessitates some order, some control of who does what, when.

There are basically three types of interpersonal relationships, based upon how control is distributed within the dyad. A dyad is a two-person system, the minimum needed for a communication-state. The three types of relationships are called symmetrical, complementary and parallel.*

Symmetrical Relations

Symmetrical relations are based on the belief that both persons have an equal right to define their relationship in all areas. Each participant says, essentially, "I have just as much right to define us as you do." Put another way, symmetrical transactions are "characterized by equality and the minimization of difference" in the control of dimension of the dyad (Watzlawick et al., 1967, pp. 68–69).

The most frequent command message observed in symmetrical relations is the "I am as good as you are," or "You can't tell me what to do," type of message. The particular issue being discussed is irrelevant to the pair. The topic of conversation is irrelevant in deciding who is to control, since both persons believe they have an equal right to assert control on all content areas. Since all activities of the two persons are open to negotiation, there is the ever-present danger of extreme competitiveness in symmetrical relations. For instance, the following symmetrical exchange was recently overheard in a restaurant between husband and wife celebrating their tenth wedding anniversary:

---

*The reader is referred to Ericson and Rogers (1973) for a description of their transactional coding scheme. They have operationalized nine different transacts that can be observed in verbal behavior.

Wife: "What do you think you'll have, Darling?"

Husband: (contemplatingly) "Well, you know I like seafood, and this place is supposed to have good seafood. So, I think I'll have my favorite—lobster."

Wife: (firmly) "But, the king crab is actually better. That's what the gourmets of seafood would eat, and besides, it's less expensive."

Husband: (defensively) "Look, I like lobster. I don't like crab. Besides, you have to crack open the crab legs, but lobster can be peeled right off the tail."

Wife: (snobbishly) "If you weren't so middle-class and dull, you'd know what's good and would order what the experts do."

Husband: (angrily) "I'll order what I damn well please. Neither you nor your so-called experts can tell me what to eat."

Wife: (haughtily) "Somebody's got to tell you what to do. With your tastes, I'm surprised you're not having peanut butter sandwiches!"

Husband: (threateningly) "Our tenth could be our last, you know."

Wife: (sarcastically) "Promises, promises!"

The rest of the meal was spent in controlled silence and rigid movement, except in the case of the bottle of burgundy drunk by the husband—they also couldn't agree on whether white or red wine goes with the lobster and crab ordered.

Having equal control in all areas may be mistakenly believed to be the ideal type of relationship, but instead, it is actually the most fragile and potentially dangerous. It is fragile because each situation must be discussed and negotiated to determine what should be done, when it should be done, and by whom. This constant negotiation would require an extraordinary amount of mutual respect, trust and tolerance of difference, if this delicate balance of equal right to determine the relationship is to be maintained.

The danger of symmetrical relations is the consistent possibility that "attempts to prove equality often end in open hostilities" (Lederer and Jackson, 1968, p. 163). In the above conversation, divorce was openly threatened and the challenge accepted. It's as if one person says to the other, "You don't scare me; I can hurt." The other replies, "You don't scare me either, since I can hurt you even more." With both persons trying to show they have at least equal right to control, they may one day have to show how equal they are and go to battle. (There is a direct analogy to the world arms race, or to management-labor relations, or to black-white issues contained in this discussion of runaway symmetrical relations.)

Calling these competitive symmetrical exchanges status struggles, Lederer and Jackson suggest the following:

> The process of the status struggle . . . usually starts when one person states or indicates an opinion, or specifies the way something should be done, or unilaterally initiates an action which involves both parties. The other person receives the message and—either consciously or unconsciously—concludes, "My spouse doesn't believe I am as competent or as good or as skilled as he is. I don't like that. I am equal." This conclusion frequently has a postscript: "I am equal—and probably superior."

> In marriage, the status struggle ("I am just as good as you are") is easily identified by the back-and-forth arguments and interruptions of the spouses. This struggle to establish an apparent equality indicates fear of inferiority, or to be more precise, it indicates a fear that the other person does not consider one his equal.
> (Lederer and Jackson, 1968, p. 164)

Even though the above quote refers to marital partners, the ideas expressed apply equally well to any interpersonal transaction. The perception that one is viewed as one-down (or inferior) to the other can occur in relations between roommates, friends, brothers, spouses, next-door-neighbors ("after all, we must keep up with the Joneses"), fellow workers, dates, etc.

Little understanding is likely in these interactions since neither person is concerned with how each interprets what the other is saying. Instead, both are concerned with how the other views himself in relations with them. The concern is not with how you see X, but with how you see me in relation to you. Messages in these symmetrical transactions tend, then, to reject the other person's point-of-view, since the attempt is to be viewed as equal to the other, and not to understand the other. Frequent status struggles are not likely to lead to open, honest messages where understanding and a communication-state emerge.

Complementary Relations

Another major type of interpersonal relations is termed complementary. This type of transaction is based on the "maximization of difference" (Watzlawick et al., 1967, p. 69).

In this kind of relationship the two persons' behaviors mutually complement or enhance each other (Lederer and Jackson, 1968). When one party wants to initiate plans and activities, the other accepts the definition and suggestions offered. In essence, the major type of command messages sent are "I'm in charge, now" and "That's fine with me." For instance, the boy calls his girl and says, "Let's go to the movies tonight and then have pizza and beer at Tony's later." The girl replies, "That sounds fine." Or, a friend calls and says, "Let's play some handball at 4 o'clock," to which you respond, "Great, I'll meet you there." Or, one person, in effect, declares, "I want to talk with someone right now. Don't criticize me now because I need to be accepted and reassured," and the friend silently listens to the troubles of the other. In each case, one person has suggested what the two of them will do, and the other has accepted or submitted to that plan.

This kind of arrangement is generally more harmonious and functional than the symmetrical pattern described earlier. Collaboration and coordination of activities are easier to attain and maintain in a complementary relationship, because each person has agreed to the manner in which they will relate to the other. A complementary relationship fits the traditional concept of a husband-wife relationship, in which "the male takes the lead by contributing the major share of ideas, and the female does her part by reacting to his suggestions, by smoothing over the rough spots, etc." (Heiss, 1962, p. 197). Interestingly enough, only about 25 percent of the couples interviewed in my own research fit this pattern (Millar, 1973). Slightly better than 50 percent of the couples interviewed actually reversed the traditional concept and the female was the one who predominantly initiated ideas and controlled the couple's conversations, while the husband smoothed over the rough spots. The dominating-husband-and-the-submitting-wife concept of marriage, then, may be another social myth which ought to be questioned and dispelled.

The danger of this type of transactional pattern is that over time and situations, the same person may always take control: the relationship becomes rigid and stagnant. Rather than alternating the control as a function of situations, skills, competencies, etc., the same person always dictates and the other always submits to those commands. Rather than temporary alternations in who controls, a pattern develops where "sustenance and protection" are provided in exchange for "compliance and appreciation" (Mills, 1967, p. 123).

A girl must consistently comply with her boy friend's suggestions not because she agrees with them, nor because she accepts his right to govern, but because she is demanding the right to be protected, to be governed, and to be dependent. In effect, she is denying her right to be a separate, responsible individual and is forcing her boy friend to define and maintain her individuality for her. Both persons in this kind of relation lose their freedom to choose how to behave, since one always submits, and the other always dominates. Also, break-up is emotionally devastating because one's self-definition is endangered.

INSIGHT 8.3   From *The Sane Society* by Erich Fromm*

What is modern man's *relationship to his fellow man?* It is one between two abstractions, two living machines, who use each other. The employer uses the ones whom he employs; the salesman uses his customers. Everybody is to everybody else a commodity, always to be treated with a certain friendliness, because even if he is not of use now, he may be later. There is not much love or hate to be found in human relations of our day. There is, rather, a superficial friendliness, and a more than superficial fairness, but behind the surface is distance and indifference. There is also a good deal of subtle distrust. When one man says to another, "You speak to John

Smith; he is all right," it is an expression of reassurance against a general distrust. Even love and the relationship between sexes have assumed this character . . . (p. 139).

What is the relationship of *man toward himself?* I have described elsewhere this relationship as "marketing orientation." In this orientation, man experiences himself as a thing to be employed successfully as the bearer of human powers. He is alienated from these powers. His aim is to sell himself successfully on the market. His sense of self does not stem from his activity as a loving and thinking individual, but from his socio-economic role. If things could speak, a typewriter would answer the question "Who are you?" by saying "I am a typewriter," and an auto-mobile by saying "I am an automobile," or more specifically by saying, "I am a Ford," or "a Buick," or "a Cadillac." If you ask a man "Who are you?", he answers "I am a manufacturer," "I am a clerk," "I am a doctor" —or "I am a married man," "I am the father of two kids," and his answer has pretty much the same meaning as that of the speaking *thing* would have. That is the way he experiences himself, not as a man, with love, fear, convictions, doubts, but as that abstraction, alienated from his real nature, which fulfills a certain function in the social system. His sense of value depends on his success: on whether he can sell himself favorably, whether he can make more of himself than he started out with, whether he is a success. His body, his mind and his soul are his capital, and his task in life is to invest it favorably, to make a profit of himself. Human qualities like friendliness, courtesy, kindness, are transformed into commodities, into assets of the "personality package," conducive to a higher price on the personality market. If the individual fails in a profitable investment of himself, he feels that *he* is a failure; if he succeeds, *he* is a success. Clearly, his sense of his own value always depends on factors extraneous to himself, on the fickle judgment of the market, which decides about his value as it decides about the value of commodities. He, like all commodities that can-not be sold profitably on the market, is worthless as far as his exchange value is concered, even though his use value may be considerable.

The alienated personality who is for sale must lose a good deal of the sense of dignity which is so characteristic of man even in most primitive cultures. He must lose almost all sense of self, of himself as a unique and induplicable entity. The sense of self stems from the experience of myself as the subject of *my* experiences, *my* thought, *my* feeling, *my* decision, *my* judgment, *my* action. It presupposes that my experience is my own, and not an alienated one. *Things* have no self and men who have become things can have no self (pp. 141–143).

* Erich Fromm, *The Sane Society* (New York: Rinehart and Company, 1955), pp. 139 and 141–143.

Perhaps the classic example of this type of complementary relationship is that between parent and child. Infancy and childhood are states of dependency, which can become rigid, so that neither is free to be. The parent, in effect, says, "I will protect, feed, clothe, and love you." The child says in return, "I will obey, appreciate and love you." The parent becomes dependent upon the child to fulfill nurturant needs, and the child becomes dependent upon the parent to sustain himself. Neither allows the other to grow, change, and develop into a responsible individual, but both become locked into a self-perpetuating, stagnating pattern. In some cases the apron strings are never cut, and neither person is allowed to develop in ways that don't maintain their rigid dependency.

The inability to readily allow for change and development is the main problem with rigid complementary relations. The one-up person will not have all the answers all the time. No matter how bright, sensitive, and well-rounded the person is, information unknown to him will be available that would be useful to the decision. If the one-up person does not allow others to periodically share in the decision-making, inappropriate decisions are bound to be made, and defensive, manipulative message styles become inevitable.

On the other hand, if the one-down person doesn't share the control aspects of the relationship once in awhile, his own ability to develop, mature, and change is severely limited. He becomes unaccustomed to thinking for himself, exploring his own feelings, and sharing himself with others.

People, circumstances, and events change over time. These changes must be dealt with honestly and openly, not forced into a previous mold which may be dysfunctional and debilitating. Children grow up and can no longer be cuddled and lavishly protected. Unexpected medical expenses force the wife to take a job, and her work gives her a renewed sense of individuality and vitality which affects relations within the household. High school friends who go off to separate colleges appear to become "different persons," and indeed, they are. These differences in skills, competencies, events, and situations will bring about changes in the way two persons relate. If these changes—however minimal they appear—are not explored and understood by the parties, then interpersonal distance, defensiveness and an inability to communicate are likely to develop, no matter how satisfactory the relationship once was.

Parallel Relations

A type of interpersonal relationship that more readily allows for change, that encourages the process of growth is called Parallel. Such a transactional pattern is more give-and-take than the other two and is the most workable, durable form of dyadic relation (Lederer and Jackson, 1968, p. 169). Instead of being primarily competitive (like the symmetrical pattern), or rigid and stagnating (like the complementary transactions), a parallel relationship is characterized by development and change within the context of mutual respect, trust, and the tolerance of differences.

In this kind of relation, the two persons have worked out their separate areas of control in which each defers to the other. They also have issues over which they share control of their relationship. For instance, the wife may have the final say on household jobs, care of the children, budget, and social engagements; the husband is in charge of the maintenance of the car, of the lawn, and of choosing vacation sites. Together, they decide where they will live, whether they should change or keep their jobs, and how often they should pursue their own separate interests and hobbies. These latter decisions may result in occasional status struggles, as when the husband plays golf too often, or the wife spends too much time with the school committee. But, these struggles rarely end in long-lasting hostilities and resentment. Since the couple has enough mutual respect for and trust in each other, some kind of workable arrangement comes out of their competitive exchanges, satisfying them both.

Whereas the predominantly symmetrical relation looks outward in separate directions, and the rigid complementary relation looks backward together to what was, the parallel pair looks outward together in the same direction. They are not overly concerned with thoughts of "what is" to the exclusion of "what could be," nor are they blinded by "what was" and therefore "should continue to be." Rather, they are oriented toward enjoying the present, building for the future, and learn-

193

ing from the past. They do not want to preserve "what was" just because it was, nor do they want to destroy the future by making every decision a win-at-all-costs battle. They have learned to negotiate workable and mutually satisfactory patterns that provide predictability and security, while still maintaining enough flexibility so that changes can occur without totally disrupting their relationship. All-or-nothing statements are not frequently observed in these couples' interactions; but when they are present, these pronouncements determine the limits of bargaining and do not function as threats or intimidations.

These individuals care enough to be open with each other, realizing that a relationship must be constantly worked at to be maintained. They have respect for each other's abilities and are tolerant of differences. Realizing that differences in opinion and conflict are inevitable, they are neither afraid of nor encourage conflict, rather, they deal with those differences by honestly trying to understand the other and to work out mutually satisfactory solutions. They trust each other enough to take risks, to allow for change and exploration, rather than repeatedly clinging to "what was." In our rapidly changing society, in which events and interpersonal relations may last but briefly, the parallel transaction seems to be the most well-suited for mutual satisfaction and actualization.

WAYS TO OVERCOME THE MYTH

1. Take responsibility for the relationships you have with others. Part of that responsibility must be the awareness that you *do* influence and control the lives of others through the relationships you form with them. As long as one denies his influence over others, he also denies his individuality—the right to be an active agent who creates his own world. As long as one denies his influence over others, he also rejects his involvement with others—the opportunity to "get into" the other person.

2. Behave in an active manner. When we believe we have no control, we become reactors, responding to what others do and say. A person who recognizes that he influences others can be-

come an actor, one who initiates actions, rather than merely responding. An actor realizes that by doing nothing, he lets the other person determine the relationship and assume the responsibility for it. When the actor initiates, he assumes control and responsibility for his own relationships. When two people act in an atmosphere of openness and trust, knowing each influences the other and assuming responsibility for that influence, then an interpersonal relationship can be negotiated with the occasional occurrence of a communication-state.

We are not arguing for you to become a "bull" in a human relationship. Bulls don't negotiate; they dominate. Bulls don't assume responsibility for relationships; they take from others without concern for consequences. The key to becoming an active person is the phrase, "within an atmosphere of openness and trust." Bulls have no awareness of the meaning of that phrase, but people do. So, overcome the myth by acting, by initiating, by being open with others, by trusting them, and by being trustworthy. If someone suggests that you do something and you have reason *not* to do it, say so! Then suggest an alternative. Find out why the other made the suggestion, and see if you can find some activity in which you both want to participate, and which achieves the same goal:

"Let's go play tennis."

"I'm not very good at tennis. Why do you want to play tennis?"

"It's a beautiful day, and I'd like to be outside."

"Well, would you like to bike-hike? We could picnic, too. That gets us outside . . . together."

3. Share the consequences for the actions within the relationship. That may mean saying "I'm sorry." It may also mean *not* demanding an apology. Transactions are mutual—one of the members of the pair is never *the* cause—both members assume responsibility and create an atmosphere of openness and trust.

4. Blindfold a partner. With your partner holding on to your elbow, walk for 15 minutes around the campus: then switch places. Once you have returned to your starting point, talk about

how you felt. Were you each afraid? when? what happened to dispel the fear, if it was dispelled? Experiencing this dependency upon another may help you understand the notion of being trusting and trustworthy.

5. Form a group of 5 to 7 members. Do not choose a leader. Discuss a topic of mutual interest setting a time limit upon your discussion. When the discussion is over, ask who dominated the group, that is, who exerted the most control upon the group as it discussed the topic? If more than one, why? What did the people do, or say, that led the group to decide they "controlled?" If all members were said to control the outcome, then did all feel responsibility for the group's efforts?

a. Examine a group of which you are a member (PTA, fraternity/sorority, chess or bridge club) to see who exerts the greatest influence upon the group. Who are the greatest complainers about the direction of the group? Are these people the same? If not, who assumed the responsibility for direction? Write a brief paper in which you specify the people in control, the complainers, and how the leading group can encourage the complainers to take a more active part in the group.

6. Write a paper identifying the kinds of relationships you have with three other people. Why do you think the relationship is either symmetrical, complementary or parallel? If the relationship is not what you would like it to be, what can you do to change it? Set a strategy for change, then talk with the other person, revealing your feelings and plans.

SUMMARY

There exists a myth in our society which seems to say that we don't influence the behavior of others; maybe it means that we shouldn't influence. Our analysis suggests that the myth is false—that we *do* influence and control others, even if we try not to by doing nothing! We have suggested that by denying that we control, we place ourselves in a "one-down" position from which can grow alienation—alienation from those around us and alienation from ourselves.

Implicit in mutual control is trust. Trust develops from trustworthy behaviors and from trusting others. Trust can only exist in a relationship if both participants are trustworthy and trusting.

We have identified three main types of relationships and have shown the difference in the control aspect of each: symmetrical (equal domination), complementary (one dominates), and parallel (both dominate at different times). We have suggested that the myth can be overcome by realizing that people are interdependent and that all of us must be willing to assume our responsibility for the relationship.

In the previous pages, we have attempted to dispel a number of social beliefs or myths which researchers and scholars from several fields call into question, and which, unfortunately, large portions of our population still believe. We have contended that the behaviors and messages which stem from these beliefs prevent people from reaching communication-states; that these beliefs encourage behaviors which prevent us from sharing ourselves and growing as individuals.

We have called for a change in belief and consequent behavior. The communication-related behaviors recommended are relevant to any context where people interact—in groups, within organizations, or giving a speech before an audience. One interpersonal context, however, which is increasingly important to our own sense of well-being and self-growth is the dyad, or two-person relationship. The ability to form satisfying and rewarding relations with our steady date, parents, friends, or spouses is increasingly important in our rapidly changing, highly mobile society. We, not a group or community, are the source of our own self-actualization.

Bibliography

Addeo, E. G., and Burger, R. E. (1973). *EgoSpeak: Why No One Listens to You.* Radnor, Pa: Chilton Book Co.

———— (1974). "Yak, Yak, Yak . . . How EgoSpeak Has Ruined Our Ability to Listen." *Detroit Magazine of the Detroit Free Press.* March 17, 27–29.

———— (1974). "EgoSpeak:" *TWA Ambassador* magazine, April: 12–14, 33.

Abarbanel, J. (1972). *Redefining the Environment.* Ithaca, N.Y.: NY State School of Industrial and Labor Relations, October.

Argyle, M. (1967). *The Psychology of Interpersonal Behavior.* Baltimore: Penguin Books.

———— (1969). *Social Interaction.* New York: Atherton Press.

———— (1972). "Non-Verbal Communication in Human Social Interaction." In *Non-Verbal Communication,* R. A. Hinde, ed. Cambridge: Cambridge University Press. 243–268.

Augsburger, D. (1973). *Caring Enough to Confront: The Love-Fight.* Glendale, Calif.: A Regal Book.

Bach, G. R., and Deutsch, R. M. (1970). *Pairing.* New York: Avon Books.

Bardwick, Judith M. (1971). *Psychology of Women: A Study of Bio-Cultural Conflicts.* New York: Harper & Row, Publishers.

Barnlund, D. C., ed. (1968). *Interpersonal Communication: Survey and Studies.* Boston: Houghton Mifflin.

———— (1968). "Communication: the Context of Change." In *Perspectives on Communication,* C. E. Larson and F. E. X. Dance, eds. Milwaukee, Wis.: Speech Communication Center. 24–41.

Bateson, N. (1966). "Familiarization, Group Discussion, and Risk Taking." *Journal of Experimental Social Psychology,* 2: 119–129.

"Behavior." *Time,* June 6, 1974, 19: 9.

199

Beier, Ernst G. (1974). "Nonverbal Communication: How We Send Emotional Messages." *Psychology Today,* vol. 8, No. 5: 52-53, 55-56.

Bennis, W. G.; Schein, E. H.; Steele, F. I.; and Berlew, D. E., eds. (1968). *Interpersonal Dynamics: Essays and Readings on Human Interaction.* Revised ed. Homewood, Ill.: The Dorsey Press.

Bennis, W. G., and Slater, P. E. (1968). *The Temporary Society.* New York: Harper & Row.

Berlo, D. K. (1960). *The Process of Communication: An Introduction to Theory and Practise.* New York: Holt, Rinehart, and Winston.

———— (1969). Unpublished Mimeo, Michigan State University.

Berne, E. (1964). *Games People Play: The Psychology of Human Relationships.* New York: Grove Press.

———— (1966). *Principles of Group Treatment.* New York: Oxford University Press.

Bickman, L. (1974). "Social Roles and Uniforms: Clothes Make the Person." *Psychology Today,* April 7, No. 11: 49-51.

Birdwhistell, R. (1952). *Introduction to Kinesics,* photo-offset. Foreign Service Institute, Louisville: University of Louisville Press.

———— (1970). *Kinesics and Context: Essays on Body Motion Communication.* Philadelphia: University of Pennsylvania Press.

Blumer, H. (1962). "Society as Symbolic Interaction." In *Human Behavior and Social Processes,* A. M. Rose, ed. Boston: Houghton Mifflin: 179-192.

Brown, C. T., and Keller, P. W. (1973). *Monologue to Dialogue: An Exploration of Interpersonal Communication.* Englewood Cliffs, N.J.: Prentice-Hall.

Brown, D. (1971). *Bury My Heart at Wounded Knee. An Indian History of the American West.* New York: Holt, Rinehart, and Winston.

Brown, R., and Ford, M. (1961). "Address in American English." *Journal of Abnormal and Social Psychology,* 62: 375-385.

Bruner, J. R. (1958). "Social Psychology and Perception." In *Readings in Social Psychology,* E. E. Maccoby; T. M. Newcomb; and E. L. Hartley, eds. New York: Holt, Rinehart, and Winston: 85-94.

Buber, M. (1958). *I and Thou,* 2nd ed. New York: Charles Scribner's Sons.

Byrne, D.; London, S.; and Reeves, K. (1968). "The Effects of Physical Attractiveness. Sex and Attitude Similarity on Interpersonal Attraction." *Journal of Personality,* 36: 259-272.

Caplow, T. (1968). *Two Against One: Coalitions in Triads.* Englewood Cliffs, N.J.: Prentice-Hall.

Carson, R. C. (1969). *Interaction Concepts of Personality.* Chicago: Aldine.

Cathcart, R. S., and Samovar, L. A., eds. (1970). *Small Group Communication: A Reader.* Dubuque, Ia.: W. C. Brown.

Cherry, C. (1966). *On Human Communication: A Review, A Survey, and A Criticism.* 2nd ed. Cambridge, Mass.: The M.I.T. Press.

Civilkly, J. M., ed. (1974). *Messages: A Reader in Human Communication.* New York: Random House.

Clevenger, T. (1959). "What is Communication?" *Journal of Communication*, 9: 5.

Cohen, A. M. (1962). "Changing Small-Group Communication Networks." *Administrative Science Quarterly*, 6: 443–462.

Cohen, A. R. (1958). "Upward Communication in Experimentally Created Hierarchies." *Human Relations*, 11: 41–54.

Cozby, P. C. (1973). "Self-Disclosure: A Literature Review." *Psychological Bulletin*, 73–91.

Dance, F. E. X., ed. (1967). *Human Communication Theory: Original Essays.* New York: Holt, Rinehart and Winston.

Davis, F. (1972). "Every Little Movement Has A Meaning All Its Own." *Woman's Day*, September, 64: 116–118.

Davitz, J. R. (1964). *The Communication of Emotional Meaning.* New York: McGraw-Hill.

Deutsch, M. (1958). "Trust and Suspicion." *Journal of Conflict Resolution*, 2: 265–279.

———— (1960a). "Trust, Trustworthiness, and the F Scale." *Journal of Abnormal and Social Psychology*, 61: 138–140.

———— (1960b). "The Effect of Motivational Orientation upon Trust and Suspicion." *Human Relations*, 13: 123–140.

Deutsch, M., and Krauss, R. (1962). "Studies of Interpersonal Bargaining." *Journal of Conflict Resolution*, 6: 52–76.

Dowling, C. (1972). "The Clothing Game." *Family Circle*, June: 18–22.

Duncan, H. D. (1967). "The Search for a Social Theory of Communication in American Sociology." In *Human Communication Theory: Original Essays*, F. E. X. Dance, ed. New York: Holt, Rinehart and Winston: 236–263.

Duncan, S. (1969). "Non-verbal Communication." *Psychological Bulletin*, 72: 116–137.

Egan, G. (1970). *Encounter: Group Processes for Interpersonal Growth.* Belmont, Calif.: Brooks/Cole.

———— (1971). *Encounter Groups: Basic Readings.* Belmont, Calif.: Brooks/Cole.

Eisenberg, A. M., and Smith, R. R. (1971). *Nonverbal Communication.* Indianapolis, Ind.: Bobbs-Merrill.

Ekman, P., and Friesen, W. (1961). "Constants Across Cultures in the Face and Emotion." *Journal of Personality and Social Psychology*, 17: 124–129.

———— (1969). "Nonverbal Leakage and Clues to Deception." *Psychiatry*, 32: 88–106.

———— (1969). "The Repertoire of Nonverbal Behavior: Categories, Origins, Usage and Coding." *Semiotica*, 1: 49–98.

Ekman, P.; Friesen, W.; and Ellsworth, P. (1971). *Emotion in the Human Face: Guidelines for Research and an Integration of Findings.* New York: Pergamon Press.

Ericson, P. M. (1972). "Relational Communication: Complementarity and Symmetry and Their Relation to Dominance-Submission." Unpublished Ph. D. dissertation, Michigan State University.

Ericson, P. M., and Rogers, L. E. (1973). "New Procedures for Analyzing Relational Communication." *Family Process,* 12: 245-267.

Fast, J. (1971). *Body Language.* New York: Pocket Books.

Fearing, F. (1962). "Human Communication." *AV Communication Review,* 10: 78-108.

Felipe, N. (1966). "Interpersonal Distance and Small Group Interaction." *Cornell Journal of Social Relations,* 1: 59-64.

Festinger, L. (1950). "Informal Social Communication." *Psychological Review,* 57: 271-282.

Fitts, W. H. (1970). *Interpersonal Competence: The Wheel Model.* Research Monograph No. 2. Nashville: Dede Wallace Center, November.

———— (1972). *The Self Concept and Psychopathology.* Research Monograph No. 4. Nashville: Dede Wallace Center, March.

———— (1972). *The Self Concept and Performance.* Research Monograph No. 5. Nashville: Dede Wallace Center, April.

———— (1972). *The Self Concept and Behavior: Overview and Supplement.* Research Monograph No. 7. Nashville: Dede Wallace Center, June.

Fitts, W. H. et al. (1971). *The Self Concept and Self-Actualization.* Research Monograph No. 3. Nashville: Dede Wallace Center, July.

Fitts, W. H., and Hammer, W. T. (1969). *The Self Concept and Delinquency.* Research Monograph No. 1. Nashville: Dede Wallace Center, July.

Fromm, E. (1955). *The Sane Society.* New York: Rinehart & Co.

Gamson, W. A. (1961). "A Theory of Coalition Formation." *American Sociological Review,* 26: 373-382.

Gazda, G. M. (1973). *Human Relations Development: A Manual for Educators.* Boston: Allyn & Bacon.

Gibb, J. R. (1961). "Defensive Communication." *Journal of Communication,* 11, 3: 141-148.

Gibb, J. R., and Gibb, L. M. (1967). "Humanistic Elements in Group Growth." In *Challenges in Humanistic Psychology,* J. Bugental, ed. New York: McGraw-Hill. 161-170.

Giffin, K., and Patton, B. (1971). *Fundamentals of Interpersonal Communication.* New York: Harper & Row.

Ginott, H. G. (1965). *Between Parent and Child: New Solutions to Old Problems.* New York: Macmillan.

Goffman, E. (1956). *The Presentation of Self in Everyday Life.* Edinburgh: University of Edinborough Press.

———— (1963). *Behavior in Public Places.* New York: The Free Press of Glencoe.

Goldenson, R. M. (1970). *The Encyclopedia of Human Behavior,* two vols. Garden City, N.Y.: Doubleday & Co.

Grimshaw, A. D., ed. (1969). *Racial Violence in the United States.* Chicago: Aldine.

Guetzkow, H. (1965). "Communications in Organizations." In *Handbook of Organizations,* J. G. March, ed., Chapter 12. Chicago: Rand McNally.

Haley, J. (1959). "An Interactional Description of Schizophrenia." *Psychiatry,* 22: 321-332.

——— (1959). "The Family of the Schizophrenic: A Model System." *Journal of Nervous and Mental Disease,* 129: 357-374.

——— (1962). "Family Experiments: A New Type of Experimentation." *Family Process,* 1: 265-293.

Hall, E. T. (1959). *The Silent Language.* New York: Doubleday & Co.

——— (1966). "A System for the Notation of Proxemic Behavior." *American Anthropologist,* 68: 1003-1026.

——— (1969). *The Hidden Dimension.* Garden City, N.Y.: Anchor Books, Doubleday & Co.

Hamachek, D. E. (1971). *Encounters with The Self.* New York: Holt, Rinehart, and Winston.

Haney, W. V. (1967). *Communication and Organizational Behavior.* Homewood, Ill.: Richard D. Irwin, Inc.

Harris, T. A. (1967). *I'm OK – You're OK: A Practical Guide to Transactional Analysis.* New York: Harper & Row.

Hayakawa, S. I. (1949). *Language in Thought and Action.* New York: Harcourt, Brace and World.

Heiss, J. S. (1962). "Degree of Intimacy and Male-Female Interaction." *Sociometry,* 25: 197-208.

Hinde, R. A., ed. (1972). *Non-Verbal Communication.* Cambridge: Cambridge University Press.

Hochreich, D. J., and Rotter, J. B. (1970). "Have College Students Become Less Trusting?" *Journal of Personality and Social Psychology,* 15: 211-214.

Homans, G. C. (1961). *Social Behavior: Its Elementary Forms.* New York: Harcourt, Brace and World.

"How Weather Affects Minds." (1974). Detroit Free Press, Friday, May 10: 1a-2a.

Irvin, C. E. (1954). "Activities Designed to Improve Listening Skill." *Journal of Communication,* 4: 14-16.

Jackson, D. D. (1965). "The Study of Family." *Family Process,* 4: 1-20.

——— (1968 ed.) *Communication, Family, and Marriage.* Palo Alto, Calif.: Science and Behavior Books.

Jacobson, W. D. (1972). *Power and Interpersonal Relations.* Belmont, Calif.: Wadsworth.

Jessor R., and Feshbach, S. (1968). *Cognition, Personality and Clinical Psychology*. San Francisco: Jossey-Bass, Inc.

Johnson, D. W. (1972). *Reaching Out: Interpersonal Effectiveness and Self-actualization*. Englewood Cliffs, N.J.: Prentice-Hall.

Johnson, E., and Johnson, M., eds. (1962). *Man Alone: Alienation in Modern Society*. New York: Laurel Edition, Dell Publishing.

Johnson, K. R. (1971). "Black Kinesics–Some Non-Verbal Communication Patterns in the Black Culture." *The Florida FL Reporter*, Spring/ Fall, 57: 17-20.

Jourard, S. M. (1968). *Disclosing Man to Himself*. New York: Van Nostrand.

———— (1971). *The Transparent Self*. New York: Van Nostrand.

Katz, D. (1947). "Psychological Barriers to Communication." *The Annals of the Academy of Political and Social Science*, 250: 17-25.

Kee, H. W., and Know, R. E. (1970). "Conceptual and Methodological Considerations in the Study of Trust and Suspicion." *Journal of Conflict Resolution*, 14: 357-366.

Kelly, C. M. (1967). "Listening: Complex of Activities–and a Unitary Skill." *Speech Monographs*, 3: 455-465.

———— (1970). "Empathic Listening." In *Small Group Communication: A Reader*, R. S. Cathcart and L. A. Samovar, eds. Dubuque, Ia.: W. C. Brown. 251-259.

Keltner, J. W. (1970). *Interpersonal Speech-Communication: Elements and Structures*. Belmont, Calif.: Wadsworth.

Keniston, K. (1965). *The Uncommitted*. New York: Harcourt, Brace, Jovanovich.

Knapp, P. H., ed. (1963). *Expressions of the Emotions in Man*. New York: International Universities Press.

———— (1972). *Nonverbal Communication in Human Interaction*. New York: Holt, Rinehart and Winston.

Krout, M. (1954). "An Experimental Attempt to Determine the Significance of Unconscious Manual Symbolic Movements." *Journal of General Psychology*, 51: 296-308.

Korzybski, A. (1933). *Science and Sanity: An Introduction to Non-Aristotelian Systems and General Semantics*. Lancaster, Pa.: Science Press Printing Co.

Laing, R. D. (1970). *Knots*. New York: Vintage Books, a Division of Random House.

Laing, R. D.; Phillipson, H.; and Lee, A. R. (1966). *Interpersonal Perception: A Theory and a Method of Research*. New York: Harper & Row.

Larson, C. E., and Dance, F. E. X., eds. (1968). *Perspectives on Communication*. Milwaukee, Wis.: Speech Communication Center.

Leach, E. (1972). "The Influence of Cultural Context on Non-verbal Communication in Man." In *Non-Verbal Communication*, R. A. Hinde, ed. Cambridge: Cambridge University Press. 315-344.

Leary, T. (1955). "The Theory and Measurement of Interpersonal Communication." *Psychiatry*, 18: 147-161.

Lederer, W. J., and Jackson, D. D. (1968). *The Mirages of Marriage*. New York: W. W. Norton.

Lewis, M. (1971). "Biorhythm: How to Cope With Your Ups and Downs." *Family Circle*, Vol. 78, No. 6, June, 36, 86.

Loomis, J. L. (1959). "Communication, the Development of Trust, and Cooperative Behavior." *Human Relations*, 4: 305-315.

Luce, G. G. (1971). "Body Time: New Clues to the Mysterious Cycles in Men and Women that Control Health, Energy, Mind." *Vogue*, vol. 158, No. 8, November 1, 156-158, 172.

———— (1973). *Body Time: Physiological Rhythms and Social Stress*. New York: Bantam Books.

Luce, R., and Raiffa, H. (1957). *Games and Decisions*. New York: Wiley.

Luft, J. (1970). *Group Processes: An Introduction to Group Dynamics*. Palo Alto, Calif.: National Press Books.

Maccoby, E. E.; Newcomb, T. M.; and Hartley, E. L., eds. (1958). *Readings in Social Psychology*. 3rd ed. New York: Holt, Rinehart, and Winston.

MacDoniels, J. W.; Yarbrough, E.; Kuszmaul, C. L.; and Giffin, K. (1971). "Openness: Personalized Expression in Interpersonal Communication." Paper presented at the International Communication Association Convention, April, Phoenix.

Manis, J. G., and Meltzer, B. N., eds. (1967). *Symbolic Interaction: A Reader in Social Psychology*. Boston: Allyn & Bacon.

Mark, R. A. (1971). "Coding Communication at the Relationship Level." *Journal of Communication*, 21: 221-232.

Maslow, A. H. (1962). *Toward a Psychology of Being*. Princeton, N.J.: Van Nostrand.

McCroskey, J. C. (1972). *An Introduction to Rhetorical Communication*. 2nd ed. Englewood Cliffs, N.J.: Prentice-Hall.

Mead, G. H. (1934). *Mind, Self and Society: From the Standpoint of a Social Behaviorist*. Edited with an Introduction by Charles W. W. Morris. Chicago: University of Chicago Press.

Mehrabian, A. (1968). "Communication Without Words." From *Psychology Today* Magazine, September, by Communications/Research/Machines.

———— (1969). "Significance of Posture and Position in the Communication of Attitude and Status Relationships." *Psychological Bulletin*, 71: 359-372.

———— (1971). *Silent Messages*. Belmont, Calif.: Wadsworth.

Mellinger, G. D. (1956). "Interpersonal Trust as a Factor in Communication." *Journal of Abnormal and Social Psychology*, 53: 304-309.

Millar, F. E. (1973). "A Transactional Analysis of Marital Communication Patterns: An Exploratory Study." Unpublished Ph. D. dissertation, Michigan State University.

Miller, G. A. (1957). *Language and Communication*. New York: McGraw-Hill.

205

———— (1967). *The Psychology of Communication: Seven Essays.* New York: Basic Books.

Miller, G. R., and Steinberg, M. (1972). "Communication and Communication Relationships." Unpublished mimeo, Michigan State University.

Mills, T. E. (1967). *The Sociology of Small Groups.* Englewood Cliffs, N.J.: Prentice-Hall.

Mishler, E. G., and Waxler, N. E. (1968). *Interaction in Families: An Experimental Study of Family Processes and Schizophrenia.* New York: Wiley.

Montague, A. (1971). *Touching: The Human Significance of Skin.* New York: Perennial Library, Harper & Row.

Mortensen, C. D. (1972). *Communication: The Study of Human Interaction.* New York: McGraw-Hill.

Morris, C. (1946). *Signs, Language and Behavior.* Englewood Cliffs, N.J.: Prentice-Hall.

Mulder, M. (1960). "The Power Variable in Communication Experiments." *Human Relations,* 12: 241-256.

Mullahy, P., ed. (1967). *A Study of Interpersonal Relations.* New York: Science House.

Myers, G. E., and Myers, M. T. (1973). *The Dynamics of Human Communication: A Laboratory Approach.* New York: McGraw-Hill.

Naunton, E. (1974). "Biorhythm Cycles and Clue to Good, Bad Days?" *Detroit Free Press,* Friday, July 5, 4Ca.

Newcomb, T. M. (1953). "An Approach to the Study of Communication Acts." *Psychological Review,* 60: 393-404.

"News Line." (1974). *Psychology Today,* May 7, No. 2: 22, 27-28, 30, 101-104.

Nierenberg, G. I., and Calero, H. H. (1973). *How to Read a Person Like a Book.* New York: Pocket Books.

Olson, D. H. (1970). "Marital and Family Therapy: Integrative Review and Critique." *Journal of Marriage and the Family,* 32: 501-538.

Pace, R. W.; Peterson, B. D.; and Radcliffe, T. R., eds. (1973). *Communication Interpersonally: A Reader.* Columbus, Ohio: Charles E. Merrill.

Paige, K. E. (1973). "Women Learn to Sing the Menstrual Blues," *Psychology Today,* Vol. 7, No. 4, September, 41-43, 45-46.

Patton, B. R., and Giffin, K. (1974). *Interpersonal Communication: Basic Text and Readings.* New York: Harper & Row.

Pool, I. de Sola (1963). "The Role of Communication in the Process of Modernization and Technological Change." In *Industrialization and Society,* B. F. Hozelitz, and W. E. Moore, eds. UNESCO.

Postman, Neil, and Weingertner, C. (1969). *Teaching as a Subversive Activity.* New York: Dell Publishing Co.

Powell, J. (1969). *Why am I Afraid to Tell You Who I am: Insights on Self-awareness, Personal Growth and Interpersonal Communication.* Niles, Ill.: Argus Communications.

Prather, H. (1970). *Notes to Myself: My Struggle to Become a Person.* Moab, Utah: Real People Press.

Rapoport, A. (1960). *Fights, Games and Debates.* Ann Arbor: The University of Michigan Press.

———— (1966). *Two-Person Game Theory: The Essential Ideas.* Ann Arbor: The University of Michigan Press.

Read, W. (1962). "Upward Communication in Industrial Hierarchies." *Human Relations,* 15: 3-15.

Reich, C. A. (1971). *The Greening of America.* New York: Bantam Books.

"Revolution of Feeling." (1970). *Time,* November 9, 54-57.

Rogers, C. R. (1951). *Client-centered Therapy.* Boston: Houghton Mifflin.

———— (1961). *On Becoming a Person: A Therapist's View of Psychotherapy.* Boston: Houghton Mifflin.

———— (1965). "Dealing with Psychological Tensions." *Journal of Applied Behavioral Science,* 1: 6-25.

Rogers, L. E. (1972). "Dyadic Systems and Transactional Communication in a Family Context." Unpublished Ph. D. dissertation, Michigan State University.

Rokeach, M. (1960). *The Open and Closed Mind.* New York: Basic Books.

Rosenthal, R.; Archer, D.; DiMatteo, M. R.; Koivumaki, J. H.; and Rogers, P. L. (1974). "Body Talk and Tone of Voice: The Language Without Words." *Psychology Today,* Vol. 8, No. 4: 64-68.

Rotter, J. B. (1967). "A New Scale for the Measurement of Interpersonal Trust." *Journal of Personality,* 35: 651-665.

———— (1971). "Generalized Expectancies for Interpersonal Trust." *American Psychologist,* 26: 443-452.

Ruesch, J., and Bateson, G., eds. (1968). *Communication: The Social Matrix of Psychiatry.* New York: W. W. Norton.

Sapir, E. (1949). *Language: An Introduction to the Study of Speech.* New York: A Harvest Book, Harcourt, Brace and Co.

———— (1958). *Culture, Language and Personality.* Edited with an Introduction by David G. Mandelbaum, Berkeley, Calif.: University of California Press.

Scheff, T. J. (1967). "Toward a Sociological Model of Consensus." *American Sociological Review,* 32: 32-46.

Schelling, T. (1960). *The Strategy of Conflict.* Cambridge, Mass.: Harvard University Press.

Schleflen, A. E. (1964). "The Significance of Posture in Communication Systems." *Psychiatry,* 27: 316-331.

Schopler, J.; Gruder, C. L.; Miller, M.; and Rousseau, M. (1967). "The Endurance of Change Induced by a Reward and a Coercive Power Figure." *Human Relations,* 20: 301-309.

Schutz, W. C. (1960). *FIRO: A Three-Dimensional Theory of Interpersonal Behavior.* New York: Holt, Rinehart, and Winston.

———— (1967). *Joy: Expanding Human Awareness.* New York: Grove Press.

Shaw, M. E. (1955). "A Comparison of Two Types of Leadership in Various Communication Nets." *Journal of Abnormal and Social Psychology,* 50: 127-134.

Shostrom, E. L. (1967). *Man, the Manipulator: The Inner Journey from Manipulation to Actualization.* New York: Bantam Books.

Simmel, G. (1950). *The Sociology of George Simmel.* Translated, edited and with an Introduction by Kurt H. Wolff. New York: The Free Press of Glencoe.

Slater, P. E. (1970). *The Pursuit of Loneliness: American Culture at the Breaking Point.* Boston: Beacon Press.

Smith, A. G. (1972). "Change, Channels and Trust." Paper presented for the Rutgers Communication Colloquium Series, April.

Smith, D. H. (1973). "Communication Research and the Idea of Process." *Speech Monographs,* 39: 174-182.

Solomon, L. (1960). "The Influence of Some Types of Power Relationships and Game Strategies upon the Development of Interpersonal Trust." *Journal of Abnormal and Social Psychology,* 61: 223-230.

Sommer, R. (1969). *Personal Space: The Behavioral Basis of Design.* Englewood Cliffs, N.J.: Prentice-Hall.

Spiegel, J., and Machotka, P. (1974). *Messages of the Body.* New York: The Free Press.

Stewart, J., ed. (1973). *Bridges not Walls: A Book about Interpersonal Communication.* Reading, Mass.: Addison-Wesley.

Sullivan, H. S. (1953). *An Interpersonal Theory of Psychiatry.* New York: W. W. Norton.

Swensen, C. H. (1973). *Introduction to Interpersonal Relations.* Glenview, Ill.: Scott, Foresman and Co.

Szasz, T. W. (1961). *The Myth of Mental Illness: Foundations of a Theory of Human Conduct.* New York: Paul B. Hoeber.

Taylor, A. B. (1965). "Role Perception, Empathy and Marriage Adjustment." *Sociology and Social Research,* 49: 22-31.

Terwilliger, B. F. (1968). *Meaning and Mind: A Study in the Psychology of Language.* New York: Oxford University Press.

Thayer, L. (1967). "Communication and Organization Theory." In *Human Communication Theory: Original Essays,* F. E. X. Dance, ed. New York: Holt, Rinehart and Winston. 70-115.

———— (1968). *Communication and Communication Systems.* In *Organization, Management, and Interpersonal Relations.* Homewood, Ill.: Richard D. Irwin.

"The Body" (1969). *Time,* June 13, 86.

"The Happy American Body, A Survey Report." (1973). *Psychology Today,* Vol. 7, No. 6, November, 119-123, 126-131.

Thibaut, J. W., and Kelley, H. H. (1959). *The Social Psychology of Groups.* New York: Wiley.

Thompson, W. (1972). *Correlates of the Self Concept.* Research Monograph No. 6. Nashville: Dede Wallace Center, June.

Toffler, A. (1971). *Future Shock.* New York: Bantam Books.

Tompkins, S. S., and Izard, C. E. (1965). *Affect, Cognition and Personality.* New York: Springer.

Wallach, M. A.; Kogan, N.; and Bem, D. J. (1962). "Group Influence on Individual Risk Taking." *Journal of Abnormal and Social Psychology,* 65: 75-86.

——— (1964). "Diffusion of Responsibility and Level of Risk Taking in Groups." *Journal of Abnormal and Social Psychology,* 68: 263-274.

Watzlawick, P.; Beavin, J. H.; and Jackson, D. D. (1967). *Pragmatics of Human Communication.* New York: W. W. Norton.

Waxler, N. E., and Mishler, E. G. (1970). "Experimental Studies of Families." In *Advances in Experimental Social Psychology,* L. Berkowitz, ed. New York: Academic Press. 5: 249-304.

Weaver, C. H. (1972). *Human Listening; Processes and Behavior.* Indianapolis, Ind.: Bobbs-Merrill.

Weaver, W. (1964). *The Mathematical Theory of Communication.* Urbana, Ill.: University of Illinois Press.

Weick, K. E. (1969). *The Social Psychology of Organizing.* Reading, Mass.: Addison-Wesley.

Wells, W., and Siegel, B. (1961). "Stereotyped Somatypes." *Psychological Reports,* 8: 77-78.

Wenburg, J. R., and Wilmot, W. W. (1973). *The Personal Communication Process.* New York: Wiley.

White, L. A. (1957). "The Symbol." In *Sociological Theory: A Book of Readings,* L. A. Coser and B. Rosenberg, eds. New York: Macmillan. 32-40.

Whorf, B. L. (1956). *Language, Thought and Reality.* Edited with an Introduction by John B. Carroll. New York: Wiley.

Williams, R. L. (1974). "Try the S.O.B. Test." *Psychology Today,* Vol. 7, No. 12, May, 101.

Winter, W. D., and Ferreira, A. J. (1969). *Research in Family Interaction.* Palo Alto, Calif.: Science and Behavior Books.

Winthrop, H. (1963). "Blocked Communication and Modern Alienation." *Journal of Humanistic Psychology,* 3: 98-111.

Zetterberg, H. L. (1965). *On Theory and Verification in Sociology.* 3rd ed. Totowa, N.J.: Bedminster Press.

Zunin, L., and Zunin, N. (1972). *Contact: The First Four Minutes.* New York: Ballantine Books.

Notes